The Gift of Administration

The Gift of Administration

Thomas C. Campbell
and
Gary B. Reierson

The Westminster Press
Philadelphia

Published by The Westminster Press®
Philadelphia, Pennsylvania

PRINTED IN THE UNITED STATES OF AMERICA

9 8 7 6 5 4 3 2

Library of Congress Cataloging in Publication Data

Campbell, Thomas Charles, 1929–
The gift of administration.

Includes bibliographical references.
1. Church management—Addresses, essays, lectures.
I. Reierson, Gary B., 1948– joint author.
II. Title.
BV652.C28 262′.1 80–24594
ISBN 0–664–24357–6

Hence I remind you to
rekindle the gift of God that is within you
through the laying on of my hands;
for God did not give us a spirit of timidity
but a spirit of power
and love
and self-control.
Do not be ashamed then . . .

II Tim. 1:6–8

Now you are the body of Christ . . .
and God has appointed in the church . . .
administrators. . . .

I Cor. 12:27–28

To
Donna
Karen
Pam

Contents

Preface

This book originated with the invitation of the faculty of Union Theological Seminary of Richmond, Virginia, to Thomas C. Campbell to give the James Sprunt lectures in 1979. His serious illness and eventual death prevented him from delivering the lectures in person (Dr. H. Wilson Yates did that) and from completing the manuscript for publication (which it was my privilege to do).

It is my personal pleasure now to thank those institutions and individuals who contributed to the completion of this project. Their number is too long to list all who supported us in this venture, but a few deserve special mention. First and foremost, our thanks go to the faculty of Union Seminary whose invitation to give the James Sprunt lectures caused this important work on ministry and administration to take place. The faculty and trustees of United Theological Seminary of the Twin Cities are to be thanked for the sabbatical leave which enabled the critical research to be done, but even more especially because United Seminary was the institution where Dr. Campbell ministered through administration and where this concept was brought to fruition. My personal gratitude goes to Plymouth Congregational Church of Minneapolis for granting me a study leave to complete the manuscript and for supporting me in my ministry and administration through the years. The Lilly Endowment, Inc., of Indianapolis, and Dr. Robert W. Lynn, Vice-President for Religion, generously supported this project in the initial stages of research and in enabling a panel of readers to consult with us before the manuscript was revised for publication.

Among the individuals deserving special thanks are these: Dr. Dayton D. Hultgren, President of United Seminary, who was Dr. Campbell's closest colleague in administration and who gave unstintingly of personal and institutional support for this work since its inception; Dr. H. Wilson Yates, whose sensitive and able presentation of the lectures and helpful suggestions were invaluable; and Dr. James M. Gustafson, Dr. Robert W. Lynn, Dr. Martin E. Marty, and Dr. James B. Nelson, all of whom read the manuscript and gave critical assistance in its revision. Special mention and thanks are extended to Ms. Shirley Schoffelman, who as Dr. Campbell's assistant was truly an administrative colleague, and Ms. Marian Hoeft, who carefully prepared the original lectures and final manuscript.

GARY B. REIERSON

Chapter I
The Gift of Administration

> And his gifts were that some should be apostles, some prophets, some evangelists, some pastors and teachers, for the equipment of the saints, for the work of ministry, for building up the body of Christ. (Eph. 4:11–12)
>
> Now you are the body of Christ . . . and God has appointed in the church . . . administrators. (I Cor. 12:27–28)
>
> Try hard to show yourself worthy of God's approval, as a labourer who need not be ashamed. (II Tim. 2:15, NEB)
>
> The problem of paperwork rather than peoplework faces me every day. A lot of days I come into the office and really feel down. All this administrative stuff is here waiting for me—stuff other people could do—when what I was trained for was the high pastoral calling of Christ to people. I sometimes think, what does all this paper have to do with Jesus? More junk for Jesus. (Interview with a minister reported in the *Minneapolis Tribune*, June 4, 1978)

In 1956, H. Richard Niebuhr's book *The Purpose of the Church and Its Ministry*[1] was published. This summary theological essay emerged from his participation in a major study of theological education in the United States and Canada. The study had been commissioned because many persons felt that there was confusion in the church regarding its ministry. Indeed, Niebuhr spoke in the book of the ministry as "the perplexed profession."[2] The essay was remarkable in many ways. One of the most remarkable things about it was that, in spite of its valuable insights, it never really brought a great deal of clarity to the confusion of the profession, and it was not widely acclaimed in the same sense that his *Christ and Culture*[3] was.

For many years the volume was out of print and has only recently been reissued. While those who commissioned his study thought there was a great deal of confusion concerning ministry prior to 1956, and Niebuhr sought to answer to the confusion, the *real* crisis in ministry was to occur following the publication rather than before. In retrospect, the 1950's seem like an era of calm and certainty rather than a period of crisis. The church and its leaders were to become caught up in broad issues of cultural upheaval during the 1960's and early 1970's. If ministers did not know what they were supposed to be doing in 1956, that feeling was to be multiplied many times over during the next twenty years. Adding to the confusion, the mainline denominations to which Niebuhr gave his main attention were experiencing numerical growth when he wrote; since that time they have known numerical and institutional decline. If leaders in a "successful" institution have a sense of uncertainty about their role, how much more is that uncertainty deepened when the institution appears to be declining?

Some observers, in reflecting about the present situation, have argued that we are now into, or moving toward, a period of calm and conservation similar to what they believe was the situation in the 1950's. This is a much too simplified analysis. While we do not have obvious cultural crises such as we have recently known in our country, it is hardly a period of calm in any profound sense. Persons do seem to have more sympathy with institutions than they appeared to have in the recent past, but only a moment's reflection produces many questions concerning the stability of our culture and its capacity to address major issues of environmental abuse, distribution of power and resources among the six continents, and confusions concerning ethical standards both within and between major cultural traditions.

The church, as one participant institution, both contributes to and reflects all of the current cultural patterns. Should its ordained leaders be stressing conservation or change? Should the church become more restrictive in its entrance requirements for leaders in the face of declining membership, or should it relax its entrance requirements while expanding its notions of mission and evangelism? What are the implications of increasing numbers preparing for ministry, especially since most of that increase is accounted for by women entering into professional ministry? Is the church an economically feasible institution as we know it? Should the church even strive to be economically feasible?

Even this brief and hardly inclusive list of issues and questions is far broader than we can hope to address in this book. However, we can attempt a theological reflection upon the ordained ministry as it is actually being practiced. What we hope to accomplish is to propose a model of ministry which will provide clergy with a solid base for addressing with the larger church the more inclusive concerns facing us all.

Our general thesis may be stated as follows: Confused contemporary usage of the traditional norms for the ordained ministry (proclamation of the gospel and administration of the sacraments) has undermined the centrality of the doctrine of the priesthood of all believers and has weakened the effectiveness of the church. Conceptualizing the definition of the clergyperson around the "gift of administration" will clarify the clergy role, support and enrich the priesthood of all believers, and strengthen the effectiveness of the church.

Before becoming more specific about the critical terms in this thesis, it is appropriate to outline certain assumptions that obviously inform much of what we will argue subsequently. These assumptions are a product of personal experience and disciplined reflection on that experience. It is a myth, which most have come to recognize, that we can divest ourselves of the biases we hold. The best we can hope for is not to achieve a disembodied expression of objective "truth," but rather to share publicly our personally perceived "truths," to test them in open debate, and then to modify, reject, or affirm them. Public expression of one's personal history and its concomitant relevant assumptions facilitates rather than inhibits productive discussion.

Our ministries—for one of us over many years in parish, teaching, and administration—have been within the broad context of the reformed, free-church tradition. We are much more informed about and committed to the reformed rather than the catholic expressions of Christianity. We are also much more convinced of the validity of the gathered-voluntary church rather than the national-parish church. We are personally more helped by those forms of worship loosely labeled "free" rather than by those forms normally called "high liturgy." We have been trained in the social sciences and have a sympathy for their contribution to theological discourse. We are suspicious of persons who claim to depend solely on Biblical or historic theological categories as the source of truth. And we are committed to the dialectical interchange between theory and practice and have little tolerance for persons who give categorical defense for either a purely deductive-rational theory of knowledge *or* a purely experiential-intuitive practical argument.

Being aware of these biases, which inform all that we do, has resulted in a more-or-less conscious attempt to try to be sensitive to places where we need to listen to those with whom we most disagree. Thus, we begin by sharing our assumptions, not to eliminate debate but to clarify and encourage it.

Multiple Expectations

Of the many ways one could describe the contemporary confusion and tension that exist among ministers, we will concentrate on two forms of the same problem: (1) multiple expectations, and (2) perceived dissonance between the ideal and the real.

Ministers, as well as many other professionals, address a large number of diverse functional expectations in the performance of their role. These expectations are found both in the mind of the person observing the minister at work and in the minister's own mind. The minister is expected to be a preacher, a liturgist, a counselor, a friend, a teacher, a social change agent, a public-spirited citizen, and a responsible parent. We could have made the list a good deal longer. Ministers may seek to order the priority of expectations by reference to the Christian tradition in which they stand and by reference to the governing board of the congregation they serve. In either case they can expect only modest help. Within the earliest Christian tradition there appears to be evidence to support multiple expectations of Christian leaders; and the normal governing board of a local congregation will have only partial sympathy for establishing priorities. Such a board will usually agree that one cannot do everything, at least not at one time, but it will rarely agree that any major item can be ignored.

To add to the tension, confusion appears in a second form: in the minister's own sense of dissonance. Ministers have a quite self-conscious sense of what they believe they ought to do and that sense of "oughtness" often appears to be in major disharmony with how they actually spend their time. The minister quoted at the beginning of this chapter had a high sense of the calling to be a Christian pastor. Instead of fulfilling that call, he saw himself spending his time "pushing papers for Jesus"! If this were an isolated case, it could be referred to a career placement counselor, but it is not an isolated instance. Competent sociologists have done several studies which show that a vast majority of the clergy see most of their actual working time devoted to functions low on their priority list. Frequently, in such studies, administration is placed at the very bottom of the list of the perceived priorities but ends up at the very top of the list of actualities. Again, to refer the problem of dissonance to the lay leadership of a congregation is not likely to result in a solution. They will agree that the minister ought not spend inordinate amounts of time in administration but should instead "be a minister." If sufficient resources are available, laity are likely to try to solve the problem of dissonance by hiring additional administrative staff.

As one seeks to bring order out of this confusion, one quickly finds that there are many strands to the web that entangles us. The strand of Christian tradition, from Biblical times down through Christian history, emphasizes not one but several major functions of ordained ministry. Certain functions appear to have had priority in different epochs. The picture is complicated when we introduce the strand of denominational particularity, which may be consistent with the epochal emphases, but more often than not is expressed in opposition to the dominant ministerial image. Focus upon social and cultural movements brings another strand into view. This forces us to recognize that ministry has never been performed in isolation from the culture in which it finds itself. In North America, especially, one finds the voluntary-gathered church existing in a political setting that holds to the principle of the separation between church and state. Considering further what we now know about personal motivation, some attention should be given to the psychological need of the clergyperson. These are only some of the most dominant strands woven together into our concerns. One could subdivide each of them until our image becomes one of a complex net surrounding us.

Any possible solution to the problems of multiple expectations and ministerial dissonance must at the very least take seriously the following areas of concern: the Biblical witness, historical Christian developments, contemporary cultural emphases, and the psychological motivations of the person engaging in ministry. As we begin our probe toward an integrated ministry we will try to take these various factors into account.

Before beginning to look for a solution to the problem outlined, we must address one other dimension of the confusion. It relates to the doctrine of the priesthood of all believers, a historic part of the Christian tradition particularly emphasized during the Reformation. The doctrine continues to be strongly affirmed by large numbers of both clergy and laity, sometimes even in the catholic tradition. It has become, however, a belief without content. We will argue that this lack of content is intimately related to the confusion concerning the role of the clergy. If the clergy are uncertain about how ministerial priorities should be ordered, it becomes even more difficult to explain how the laity are expected to be "priests." What does ordination signify that is distinct from what all lay priests do?

Since Reformation times many have sought to answer this question by the use of an ordination formula that focuses upon the faithful preaching of the gospel and the right administration of the sacraments. On the face of it, this seems to be an adequate answer, since most lay persons neither preach nor administer sacraments, and most clergy certainly do. However, a subtle distortion of the formula easily emerges. If ordained ministry is defined by what lay persons do *not* do, then as we describe what the clergy *do,* the laity are eliminated from responsibility for those functions. Thus if the ministerial functions include counseling, the laity are not expected to counsel; if the clergy are to lead worship, the laity need not. If the minister is a teacher, the lay member is not expected to teach. If the pastor becomes defined as professional friend, then the lay member is relieved of the responsibility of seeking out the lost and the lonely. For the frustrated clergyperson who was quoted earlier, it seems that the one thing the laity certainly can be expected to do is to help with the administration. *But* his complaint was that they *did not.* We often put thoughtful laity on church boards because of their secular administrative insights and discover that they seem to lose all wisdom the minute they begin to deal with *church* "business." They approve policies and make decisions that they would never permit in their workaday world. What is happening here?

We contend that the way our traditional ordination formula of word and sacrament has come to be used is a misuse. For all practical purposes, it has created a "priestly" symbol for ministry that leaves the laity without content for their own real priesthood. The church is obviously thereby weakened in effectiveness. We will give just one illustration of how this works out in practice.

Many of our denominations in America have made a conscious effort for many years to have equal representation of laity with clergy at various levels of church governing bodies. If the laity have an equal number of votes with the clergy, we feel protected against having a "priestly" caste governing our church bodies at the various levels of decision-making. In fact, these bodies have not been as representative of lay attitudes and opinions as they were designed to be. Large numbers of thoughtful lay persons have avoided such offices, believing that church business is clergy business anyway. The delegates become clergy spouses, the retired, the willing "warm body," and the eager "youth" delegate. In some denominations this pattern of subtle clerical domination is producing a reactionary trend. In the absence of meaningful definitions of the priesthood of all believers, para-organizations of ultraconservative laity and clergy are banding together to make their voices heard in the centers of power. Often such groups are far more definite about what they oppose than what they advocate.

The solution to these issues is neither simple nor magical, but it must take into account the same complexity that has produced the problematic web.

Ministry in the New Testament

No single clear pattern of formal ministry is present in the Biblical period. On this point there is general agreement among scholars who have examined the Biblical material with respect to its treatment of issues of ordained ministry. Thoughtful investigators have found evidence to support several forms of ministry and church order: episcopal, presbyterian, and congregational. Therefore, our review of the Biblical period will make no claim for a particular point of view, but will rather give attention to any major insights which do seem to be present in the texts. It will also take note of what is not said as well as what seems to be affirmed.

During the period in which the New Testament was written, institutional patterns of the Christian church were fluid. The newly emergent congregations were slowly defining their forms of leadership, and not all Christian communities followed parallel patterns. While several terms are used to refer to those performing various forms of leadership, it is not entirely clear how many terms could be applied to the same people. It seems reasonable to assume that in such a fluid period rigid distinctions had not been developed, and that it would not be unusual for the same person to fill more than one function. From evidence in I Corinthians 12 or in Ephesians 4 one might well argue that apostles, prophets, and teachers were distinct groups of persons with separate gifts and functions. Likewise, there are indications in Acts (6:2; 11:30; 14:23; etc.) of a separate group of elders appointed with distinct functions.

However, the evidence for separate persons performing distinct functions is ambiguous. In Acts 20:17 and 28 it appears that elders had functions of general oversight of congregations and were not limited to serving tables or distributing relief. In I Peter 5, also, it seems that elders have more general functions within congregations. Phil. 1:1 addresses bishops and deacons but does not mention elders. In James 5:14 elders not only visit the sick but also are those who "anoint with oil in the name of the Lord."

Probably the most developed forms for ministry are found in the pastoral epistles, but even here the pattern has ambiguities. Bishops seem to be distinguished from deacons (I Tim. 3:1 and 3:8) and perhaps elders (5:17), though there appears to be some overlap of function, for at least some elders preach and teach. Were such elders rulers *and* teacher-preachers while other elders were rulers only? The author of I Peter was certainly a teacher (preacher as well?) and considered himself an elder. His advice to fellow elders, however, sounds like counsel on pastoral care and not simply advice on legislative matters.

In the midst of the ambiguity and multiple terminology, what can be affirmed as a pattern? First of all, while the early church generally recognized several forms of leadership, not all of these took on the character of formal, recognized offices. Thus we need to distinguish between general recognition and formal recognition of different types of leadership. It appears that apostles, prophets, and teachers, while they were known and recognized, were not ordained. The apostles had a founding function with regard to churches—they were traveling evangelists or missionaries. As for the prophets and teachers, "there is no hint that these were in any way ordained men. Their ministry rested upon recognition in the church of their immediately inspired character."[4] They were highly significant functionaries, and the ranking that Paul gives them right after the apostles "was probably not a singular opinion of his own."[5] It seems most likely that such persons were not attached to particular communities. On the other hand, bishops, deacons, and elders were related to particular communities of believers and they had some formal recognition or ordination. Healers and speakers in tongues were recognized but not formally. Thus, we have two categories of leadership beginning to emerge, those formally recognized by particular congregations and those with more general recognition and function. The early church appears to have profited from both forms. Is it possible to distinguish between the two types and discover the enduring values of each?

What holds together in a single category bishops, deacons, and elders and eliminates apostles, prophets, teachers, healers, and speakers in tongues? The distinguishing factor is that the former all have some direct relation to sustaining a community. They are in some way concerned with order within the community. To be sure, their work is related to the work of the apostles, prophets, and teachers, but they focus upon concerns for community continuity and permanence which apostles, prophets, and teachers are able to ignore.

We have thus emphasized a distinction between what can be called "settled" ministries, and those ministries only tangentially related to community continuity. However, let us be clear about two matters: There is an interrelation between the two types, and *if* "priority" is given to one or the other type, Paul at least seems to favor the nonordered ministries. The case for that priority however is not totally clear. (Founding, of course, comes before maintenance, but founding without maintenance seems pointless.)

One clear omission in all of this is priests. The New Testament makes no reference to priests in connection with community leadership. Whenever the word is used, it refers either to the priesthood of Christ or to the priesthood of all believers. It never applies to the office of ministry.[6] Priesthood implies liturgical sacrifice and mediation. Such sacrifice and mediation belong in the first instance to our High Priest (Christ) and in the second instance to all believers in a derivative sense from the priesthood of Christ. Sacrifice in the form of service is the common calling for all Christians and cannot in any meaningful sense be delegated by the company of believers to the office of the ministry. Sacrifice and service are common to all believers and cannot be used to distinguish ministerial offices and functions. "If elsewhere the priest is aloof from the people, here (in Christianity) the whole new people of God is a priestly fellowship."[7]

Gifts for Ministry

Thus far we have not addressed, in any direct way, gifts as they relate to ministry. We have tended to use the terms "functions" and "gifts" somewhat synonymously. In one sense the authors of the New Testament do not use sociological categories such as "functions" or "roles," but they do see various gifts as clearly related to forms of ministry. It is therefore necessary to clarify the nature of ministerial gifts before moving on.

The New Testament affirms that all of the gifts utilized in any of the forms of ministry are gifts of the Holy Spirit and therefore should more properly be called spiritual gifts (Heb. 2:4). They take the form of both ecstatic and normal talents and activities, and they are all God-given. They are related in a derivative sense to the overall gift of grace which we have known in Jesus as the Christ.

> All spiritual gifts are valid, but not all are equally good. Their worth to the church determines their value. . . . [Paul] introduces the analogy of the body (I Cor. 12:12–26), with its organic unity, diversity of function, interdependence of members, to illustrate how the *charismata* are also diverse in function, interdependent, and designed to give unity, solidarity, and healthy growth to the Christian fellowship. All gifts, therefore, are to be subordinated to, and have value in proportion as they further, this purpose. The ministry is graciously given (Eph. 4:7–8) to bring the church "to mature manhood, to the measure of the stature of the fulness of Christ." . . . Every gift is justified in the measure that it contributes to the faith and knowledge, peace and order, of the church, and must be exercised with a deep sense of responsibility to God, who has called Christians to be "good stewards" of (God's) "varied grace" (I Cor. 14:33, 36; I Pet. 4:10–11).[8]

All of the ministerial gifts are for the "equipment of the saints, for the work of ministry, for building up the body of Christ" (Eph. 4:11–12).

Thus, while the church chose to recognize officially *some* forms of ministry, that recognition assumed that those ministries—like all of the other forms—were fundamentally empowered by the Holy Spirit. This pattern became more explicit in the period of the early church fathers and was defended by Ignatius in his threefold explication of ministry, with bishops, presbyters, and deacons.[9] He made the distinction between each of the offices more explicit than other early writers did. These three offices (whether clearly defined or not) were responsible for the sustained leadership in the early church, and received formal recognition as such.

The Reformation Emphases

The Reformation in its total range covers a wide spectrum of interpretations of ministry. From Anglicanism to radical left-wing groups, the varieties of ministerial practice and theological interpretation are significantly and meaningfully diverse. We will concentrate here upon the Calvinist and Puritan interpretations, for in one sense they represent a broad median position within the general Reformation options.

When both Luther and Calvin discussed the priesthood of all believers,[10] they were not transferring the priesthood from the priest to the laity, rather they were moving the priestly function to Christ. Christ was Prophet, Priest, and King. Such a movement could logically have resulted in a rejection of any special ministerial order, as indeed it did for many left-wing groups. However, for Calvin it meant no such thing. He and those who followed him believed that there was a clear need for a *reformed* ministerial order. With the priesthood so centrally located in Christ, there is an added need for the church to have true teaching and doctrine. To place this responsibility in some form of ministerial order has the danger of separating clergy from laity. But that risk was considered less than the risk of chaos without order, and the risk could be at least minimized by distributing responsibilities among several forms of ministerial order. When Calvin examined the Eph. 4:1–16 passage (*Institutes* IV.3.4),[11] he declared that of the five functions of ministry mentioned, only two were intended as permanent offices of ministry, namely, pastors and teachers. The other three offices, apostles, prophets, and evangelists, were of a nonsuccessive character. And while God may indeed raise up such persons from time to time, they are not to be permanently provided for within the church. The two "permanent" offices were subdivided in Calvin's church constitution into four classes: preachers, doctors, elders, and deacons.[12] The preachers, serving particular congregations, and the doctors, were to proclaim and teach the pure doctrine, while the elders and deacons were to have concern for the discipline of the congregation and the other matters of order which would be brought before the consistory. The deacons administered the contributions for the needy as well as the possessions and income of the church itself. Luther shared Calvin's concern for the matter of faithful teaching of doctrine, but had a much less developed doctrine of ministerial order.[13]

> The Reformers customarily spoke of the minister as pastor (shepherd, in relation to certain New Testament passages, e.g., John 10:2 and 10:16; Hebrews 13:20; I Peter 2:25), but they called him most frequently "preacher." . . . The term "pastor" came into general use only during the eighteenth century under the influence of Pietism, especially in Lutheranism. The German Reformers also adhered to the medieval usage and called the preacher *Pfarrer,* i.e., parson (derived from *parochia*-parish, and *parochus*-parson). The common people most generally called the ministers "preachers," but they also continued to use the terms to which they had been accustomed under Roman Catholicism, i.e., "priests," et cetera. . . . The term "minister" was gradually introduced into English-speaking countries by the Nonconformists and Dissenters. Dependent upon Calvinism, they distinguished the Protestant "ministry" from the Anglican "clergy."[14]

Faithful preaching of the gospel and correct administration of the sacraments were primary in the thought of the Reformers. However, the place of discipline and order as central ministerial functions was also emphasized, especially in the thinking of Calvin and his followers. This disciplinary function was shared by both the preachers and the elders, but was never intended to imply that the members of the consistory were *above* the congregation. They were rather *within* it. Calvin and the Calvinists were, in principle, faithful to the

Ephesian notion that all of the forms of ministry were for *building up* the body of Christ.

Calvin, the Puritan Calvinists, the Scottish followers of Knox, and the Wesleyans all had a deep sense of order and discipline related to the functions of ordained ministry. Order and discipline were ways of expressing sanctification. The Reformers were concerned that the holiness of the church be furthered. This sanctificationist element in the doctrines of ministry was susceptible to theocratic excesses; it was at the root of the witch-hunting of the later Puritans; it contributed to Wesleyan attempts to measure increases in purity. Still it was a logical and necessary concern if one wants to take seriously what it means to be faithful as a result of God's gracious gift of redemption in Jesus Christ. It is a continuing concern for how one is to serve sacrifically if the sacrifice of the High Priest is to be *e*ffective as well as *a*ffective.

Another way of stating the issue is to underline the Reformers' concern to find an effective way to preserve the doctrine of human depravity while recognizing that the new life in Christ must include some evidence of Christian perfection. Thus, ministerial discipline sought to affirm a doctrine of the human which was neither "too high" nor "too low."

Using Secular Resources

When we turn to the contemporary period in discussing the nature of ministry we find two tendencies. The first involves research focused on Biblical and historical materials, seeking increased insight into what was the pattern of ministry in the early church, or what was the pattern intended by each denomination. The second effort is to find ways to integrate contemporary secular knowledge into our understandings of ministry.

Having just briefly reviewed issues that appear to be relevant to our concerns from the Biblical and historical perspectives, we now turn to this second major contemporary tendency, namely, integrating the contributions of secular knowledge into our understandings of ministry.

Those concerned with making use of secular knowledge have tended to seek a more synoptic view of ministry incorporating both theological and secular insights. The work of H. Richard Niebuhr, already mentioned,[15] is one example. Other thinkers have made attempts to introduce valid secular insights into the performance of particular ministerial functions, for example, the integration of psychological insights into our understanding of pastoral counseling. A number of persons have also addressed the issue of "professionalization" of the ministry, making comparisons between the ministry as a profession and other professions such as law and medicine.

Debate on this issue has been extensive, heated, and sometimes profound. Have the "integrationists" enriched our understanding of ministry, or have they lost its distinctive theological understanding in seeking integration with the secular forms of knowledge? Is the psychologically trained clergyperson in essence only a poor substitute for a psychiatrist, or one who has combined psychological insight with Christian grace-filled healing? Is the trained Christian educator a person truly able to nurture the uninformed into the mysteries of the Christian faith, or one who uses educational theory and techniques either to manipulate the unsuspecting or to inoculate the faithful so that they can no longer receive the impact of full Christian conversion?

Resolution of these debates has been made more difficult because Christian scholarship itself tends to be disciplinary rather than synoptic, and because seminary curricula have for the most part been informed by a deductive theory of learning. The usual seminary program is fundamentally divided into four parts, each following somewhat deductively from the preceding: Biblical theology, historical theology, systematic theology, and practical theology.[16] It is then but a short step to transform the deductive sequence into a hierarchical ordering from highest to lowest. In some ways, this stratification is quite understandable. Culturally something like it prevails in a great number of other graduate fields, and theologically it can be argued that, particularly as Protestant Christians, we are a "people of the Word." Somehow, therefore, "education" precedes action. On the other hand, it is also a curious hierarchy to have taken place particularly in America where there is a recognized bias in favor of the "practical." Theologically, Christianity is preeminent among religions with its incarnational and actional focus.

We are not so naive as to think that we will resolve this debate. The existence of the debate and its consequences, however, are germane to what we are about. One need not employ sophisticated theories to explain why theological students, studying in a system that lifts thematical disciplines to the highest esteem, become graduates who doubt the value of their most practical efforts. The graduates are not subject to some psychological difficulty; they are simply bright people who learned the lessons they were taught, as much by the *latent* as by the manifest system, at the seminary.

One additional comment is appropriate. Max Weber made some observations regarding the differences between the scientist and the politician. The politician is granted "above all the feeling of holding in one's hands a nerve fiber of historically important events."[17] The scientist on the other hand is a "strict specialist,"[18] devoted to "science for science's sake,"[19] and "chained to the course of progress,"[20] that is, asking for one's own specialized work and knowledge to be surpassed and outdated as time moves along. Both types of persons have a calling or motivation, but each has a different content. The calling of the minister has much in common with the calling of the politician, in Weber's terms, while the seminary faculty member's calling has more in common with Weber's concept of the calling of the scientist. This difference does not fully explain all that underlies the debate concerning the value of the integration of disciplines toward the functioning of the clergyperson, but it does give some insight into why the debate persists.

In these pages we will seek integrative insight between certain theological assumptions about ministry and certain developments that have taken place in recent years in the administrative sciences. The "scientists" among our readers, whether of the theological or administrative sort, will have crucial questions to raise at several points. The "politicians," whether ministerial or executive, will be uneasy with the relative lack of extensive practical application. The scientists will question the use of certain scholarly findings and the politicians will want more examples of ways to "have a hand in history."

In a general sense this book carries further the implications of the work begun by H. Richard Niebuhr. It has the advantage of several developments within the administrative sciences which have taken place since he wrote *The Purpose of the Church and Its Ministry.* Like him, we will argue for the need to remain faithful to the tradition of the church as well as to the contemporary situation. Also, like him, we will presume that all ministerial functions are performed in the context of a group of persons (the priesthood of believers), even if the particular ministerial act is at a particular moment focused toward an individual person, as in counseling. Unlike Niebuhr, we will suggest ways in which the administrative sciences interrelate with the functions of ministry.

The Minister as Person

The motivation of the person engaged in ministry is our fourth and final general area to be noted in moving toward a solution of the problem. Historically, the focus has been on the call experienced by the person. Even today, most seminaries ask potential students to submit autobiographical essays of their personal religious pilgrimages, and denominational processes for ordination normally put considerable emphasis upon the candidate's interpretation and defense of the "secret" call to ministry.[21]

Extensive recent research on the issue of when a person is

ready for ministry[22] indicates that, in all denominations studied, personal factors rank highest in assessing readiness for ministry. An interesting dimension of this research is that those personal factors are not easily subject to "instruction." The elements that make up what the authors of the study called an "Open Affirming Style" are not readily assimilated into a seminary course of instruction. Who has notions about how one teaches "fidelity," "flexibility," "responsibility," or "positive approach"? What professor wishes to develop an introductory course on "Personal Integrity 101"?

Despite the elusive character of personal dimensions of the clergy role, everyone recognizes that such personal matters cannot be ignored. James Dittes has sought to integrate the insights of the psychological disciplines with the characteristics of the church and its ministry.[23] In his study entitled *Minister on the Spot,* he outlines a psychological profile that correlates highly with those who select the ministry as a vocation (or is it the selection of the Holy Spirit?). This profile he calls the "Little Adult."

Paul Tillich's *Systematic Theology*[24] explicitly correlates theological categories with psychological insights. While the person of the minister was not his primary concern, nevertheless in the third volume he discusses leadership of social groups (including churches) and asserts that "leadership is the social analogy to centeredness."[25] A social group, including a congregation, must be centered, and there is a sense in which the minister represents that center. We will return later to his development of this concept.

Administration: The Centripetal/Centrifugal Gift

What then have we argued thus far? Contemporary clergypersons are faced with expectations from those they serve, as well as their own self-expectations. Clergy often experience this sense of multiplicity as dissonant and disharmonious. Indeed, the disharmony may be severe in the sense that what appeared at the outset to be the central focus for their ministry often becomes in fact marginal in the way they actually spend their time.

From the review of Biblical material we see that, even in the earliest period of church history, leadership took a variety of forms, sometimes in the same person, sometimes in different groups of persons. However, only those forms of leadership which were directed at sustaining the community of believers were *formally* recognized by the community. Elders, bishops, and deacons were all of such a character. These particular "settled" ministries were, like the other forms of ministry, considered to be *gifts of the Spirit* which the church was only acknowledging through its formal recognition procedures.

In the work of the Reformers we find also that formally recognized ministries were intended for the building up of the body of believers. While word and sacrament were fundamental to their vision of ministry, attention was clearly given to issues of order and discipline in the community. The clergy were *within* the congregations to maintain the order and functioning of those congregations in a manner faithful to the gospel message. Sanctificationist implications were included in the Reformers' notions of ministry.

In the contemporary period we have seen efforts to integrate secular knowledge into our conceptions of ministry, particularly insights from the administrative sciences. If ministry is concerned finally and intentionally with *building up* the community of believers, then that branch of knowledge concerned with group leadership and coordination ought to be a prime area for integration and insight.

And finally we have noted that the *personal motivation* of the person performing ministry must be taken into account. Personal motivation includes both what ministers themselves want to do *as individuals* in ministering to others, and their willingness to be identified with *the community of believers* as the central locus for ministry.

A unifying symbol that would encourage incorporating Biblical and social science insights could assist ministers to move toward an integrated, though tension-filled, performance of their calling. Each of the Biblical terms has often been used to symbolize unity by some clergy at some point in history. Often the usage has not been consistent with the Biblical content of the term itself. Substitute terms have been used at various points, as for example the term "parson" (*the* person). Niebuhr suggested the term "pastoral director"[26] as the emerging new conception. This compound term was meant to account for the faithful use both of traditional concepts and of the contemporary realities. Legitimate as his efforts were, Niebuhr's unifying symbol failed to receive much support, and basically for four reasons: (1) his use of administrative insights was not developed in any detailed sense; (2) significant developments in administrative theory and practice were yet to be fully articulated; (3) the symbolic term was suggested just at a time when major critiques against institutionalization were being mobilized; and (4) the compound term was easily distorted into the notion of a controlling shepherd who manipulates a subordinate flock of sheep. The term "pastor" carried for many an outmoded rural imagery, while the term "director" was overlaid with the images of the "big operator" (Niebuhr himself recognized this perversion and sought to address it).[27]

Our suggestion is that a more appropriate unifying symbol is to speak of the "gift of administration" or of the minister-administrator. The call to ministry is centrally seen as a spiritual *gift, but* unlike other ministerial spiritual gifts it focuses *into and out from* the community of believers. It is intended primarily for the equipment of the saints and for building up the body of Christ. It is tested by the body and is the only form of gift which the body recognizes in any formal communal way. It is a gift which underlies every function that the minister individually performs, and yet it does not in any way undermine, but rather enhances, the priesthood of *all* believers.

It is a *centripetal* gift in the sense that those having it are constantly drawn into the centeredness of the community itself with incredible force and must in their person welcome such centering. It is a *centrifugal* gift, for, unless equally powerful forces are generated by the leadership of the community to produce acts of ministry to the world beyond the community, the result is a deadly whirlpool of self-concern and communal self-interest. The imagery of powerful forces both "pulling in" and "throwing out" is purposely chosen in order to reject any suggestion of hierarchical order to the relationships. *All* members of the community are ministers whether formally recognized as leaders or not. The powerful forces building up the body and reaching out encompass all. No one is exempt from them.

In rejecting hierarchical imagery, we can better understand the way in which Paul ordered the gifts of ministry in I Corinthians 12. The first are apostles; the second, prophets; the third, teachers; the fourth, workers of miracles; and *only then* healers, helpers, administrators, and speakers in tongues. Administration of the community is almost at the bottom of the list. In subtle ways, persons entering formally recognized ministry have been taught that they are, above all, apostles, prophets, and teachers! Such a calling may not pay very well, but it is the *first* among the gifts that need to be performed! This clerical desire for "first seats" is hardly consistent with the gospel, and yet Paul *has* given the right order of priority. How can we resolve this tension?

In commenting on this list (and the place of administration in it), Kittel makes the following observation, which is worth noting (although it may put too much weight on what Paul does *not* say):

> No society can exist without some order and direction. It is the grace of God to give gifts which equip for government. A striking point is that when in v. 29 Paul asks whether all are apostles, whether all are prophets or whether all have gifts of healing, there are no corresponding questions in respect of [helpers] and [administrators]. There is a natural reason for this. If necessary, any member of the congregation may step in to serve as deacon or ruler. Hence these offices, as distinct from those

> mentioned in v. 29, may be elective. But this does not alter the fact that for their proper discharge the *charisma* of God is indispensable.[28]

In discussing the term "administrator," Kittel points to its linguistic origin in relation to the steering of a ship. The person at the wheel is under orders, and the captain is also under orders from the owner. The administrator is the one at the wheel of the congregation. Proclamation of the Word was not originally one of the tasks for such a person; the apostles, prophets, and teachers did that.

This may indeed be making more of what Paul did not say than what he said, but nevertheless Kittel's emphasis is consonant with the argument being pursued here. The term "administrator" points to that which is *common* rather than that which is *unique.* It is that which unifies rather than that which sets apart. It is, in God's grace, a widespread gift. Let us be clear about this: all clergy are *not* prophets; all clergy are not even gifted preachers; they are not all gifted teachers. But they *can* all be gifted administrators! All can be seen as *gifted* because they alone can use *all* of *the gifts in the fellowship* as a part of their administration! Thus, they are *representative persons.* They re-present the community to the world. In this sense, the minister-administrator is a contemporary equivalent to the Puritan "parson." A. T. Hanson underlines this theme when he discusses the doctrine of ministry contained in I Cor. 3:18 to 4:16 (though Hanson does seem to make the minister more of a "model person" than we would intend):

> Consequently this whole passage I Cor. 3:18–4:16 has very great importance for Paul's doctrine of the ministry. From it we learn that the task of the ministry is to serve the Church, but to serve it by itself first living out the suffering, redeeming life of Christ in the world, in order that the Church as a whole may do likewise. We notice especially 4:16: "I beseech you therefore, be imitators of me." Thus the ministry has a double relationship: it is related to Christ as responsible to him and as being the primary means by which his life is reproduced in the world. And

> it is related to the Church as serving the Church, and as leading the Church as a whole into the same life which itself is exhibiting. There is no suggestion here of the ministry doing anything which the Church as a whole cannot do: it is rather that the ministry is the pioneer in Christian living for the Church, as Christ was the pioneer for all of us.[29]

Daniel Jenkins makes this same point when interpreting Mark 10:45 as the key text for ministry ("For the Son of man also came not to be served but to serve"). His exposition likewise indicates the role of the minister as that of "representative" person.[30]

So long as ministers see their actual activities as different from what the laity do, they necessarily encourage the laity to see the clergy as "set apart." Minister-administrators encourage the whole body of believers to see ministry *through* themselves. Often the clergy suggest that if lay persons wish to engage in ministry, they should *take time out* from normal activities to engage in specific "acts of ministry." They should volunteer to help in the hospital, lead a youth group, or assist in a specialized ministry with the dispossessed. While these are all valid extensions of ministry, they become peripheral to "normal" life and in some sense remain "special." We are suggesting that the ministry of the laity is properly carried out not in special projects but in the common things they do. Perfectly competent church members who normally function in responsible executive positions in the culture at large often become a great disappointment when appointed to church boards or church agency boards. They refuse to submit church plans to the same rigorous judgment that they normally bring into their day-to-day decision-making. Why is this? We are suggesting that the misunderstanding of ministry as something "set apart" and different has contributed to their hesitation to use their giftedness fully and freely.

Integrating Disciplines

To incorporate the insights from the administrative disciplines into the theory and practice of ministry, care must be exercised. It is always possible that underlying assumptions in one discipline are inconsistent with those of another. One cannot readily import techniques and practices developed in one sphere of life into another sphere without the underlying assumptions being imported along with the practice. These are the problems that beset us in developing a coherent theology of ministry which desires to use secular insights without becoming controlled by them. Let us clarify what we are *not* doing in integrating these disciplines.

First of all, we are not arguing simply that churches should become more "businesslike." That is to say, churches and their ordained clergy will not necessarily become more faithful to their calling by seeking to become more efficient. Nor will they become more appropriate instruments of God's action by measuring success through profit-and-loss statements.

Secondly, we are not simply arguing that it would be helpful to the church to introduce useful management tools developed in the secular order. After all, some tasks in the church parallel those in the business world, so we can profitably use the techniques others have developed. This subtle suggestion has a limited utility, and some helpful books have been based on that particular argument.[31] However, there are reasons for rejecting the argument in its simplest form. It is a rare technique that does not have underlying assumptions that support it. These assumptions may or may not be ones that the church would find coherent with its own self-understandings. For example, several techniques of business control assume that total authority for operations is lodged in the chief executive officer. Everyone involved has accepted that assumption. To apply techniques based on that assumption in most local Protestant congregations would distort much that we have already said about the nature of the Christian community of believers. Another reason for caution in using management tools and techniques in the church is that such techniques are often interrelated. One cannot pick and choose at random, for many techniques will not function if applied in isolation. For example, written job descriptions as a technique of control assume that there is a review process, a clear line of accountability, and adequate measures for judging performance. More than a few ministers have worked out clear job descriptions with chairpersons of the board only to find that other board members did not agree with the descriptions and none of them knew just how they were going to measure adequate performance. It would have been far better not to have had a job description, for then at least everyone would have known that the task was nebulous and subject to many interpretations.

Thirdly, we are not beginning with a particular management theory that we want to play back against some "proof texts" from the Christian tradition on the nature of ministry. It is our assumption that no two major fields of endeavor ever neatly and precisely interrelate. Finally, "no one can serve two masters." Thus, while we will make every effort to search for places of coherence and compatibility between our theological understandings of ministry and insights from particular schools of management theory, when there is conflict it will be resolved by theological appeal and not by administrative consistency. It is *ministry through administration* we are primarily discussing and not leadership of social groups in general or of capitalistic businesses in particular.

Finally, we are not attempting to relate all of the major ecclesiological options to a range of management theories. That task has already been done with considerable helpfulness by Peter Rudge.[32] He emphasized the possible options for relationship between doctrines of ministry and management theories. We are assuming Rudge's work and developing one of his major options.[33]

Only one broad theological option is being considered here in detail. It focuses on the central elements of the Reformation theories of ministry which correlate with the position Niebuhr has labeled as "Christ the Transformer of Culture." In the Reformation period this position was represented in Calvin and his immediate followers such as Knox. During the English Reformation this broad tradition was represented in the Puritans and Separatists as well as in the Wesleyans. In the contemporary period, modern exponents of this tradition include such theologians as H. Richard Niebuhr and Paul Tillich. Reinhold Niebuhr obviously also stands in this broad stream of thought, but he did almost no constructive work on the nature of the church.

These theological commitments will in all cases take precedence in choosing themes to be addressed and will govern choices which need to be made with respect to the use of administrative theory and practices. The transformative position toward culture cannot automatically cause one to reject secular forms of thought as inconsistent with the Christian tradition. In fact, such a position enables one to see both symbolic and practical import in many secular areas of knowledge. Furthermore, from this general theological position one can also reject with some ease certain management schools as having little value for the church and its ministry. For example, the so-called "classical school" of management gives too much power to persons in leadership positions without any check being imposed upon that power. The classical school assumes too high a doctrine of the human for those in leadership positions.

Transformists would have reservations about the unqualified use of the "human relations school." Advocates of the human relations position have indeed seen the need to limit the power and authority of the hierarchy, but are they unrealistic about human nature? In incorporating many pure democratic elements into administrative functioning are they in danger of having too high a doctrine of the human in general? Transformists would also worry that "human relations experts" might be tempted into subtle forms of manipulation and thereby become a greater danger than autocrats, about whom we are at least clear what they are trying to do! Even the "systemic school" is not without critique from the transformists' point of view. Can the human mind ever really know the full "system" under which we all function? Do certain systemic models not presume that there is a fully determined character to reality, and are they tempted to seek the elimination of human freedom and the wonderful sense of creative serendipity?[34]

Equipping and Building Up

The subsequent chapters will focus upon four central terms that explain the content of the gift of administration: stewards, elders, bishops, and deacons. Each term focuses upon a critical aspect of the ministry, an aspect that must be performed with integrity if the body of believers is to be equipped and built up. Together they are meant to be inclusive and exhaustive. If the task before us is done well, there should be no major aspect of ministry through administration which is ignored or left untouched.

Theologically we will examine the tensions under which each aspect of ministry is performed. Also, each of our four terms will be examined in relation to the way a particular Gospel deals with the life and ministry of Jesus Christ. Stewards, elders, bishops, and deacons are all minister-administrators, but each represents a somewhat distinct aspect of ministry. Three of the four focus terms are applied to laity as well as clergy. This is as it should be!

We will use much of what has been learned in the secular administrative disciplines, and we will interrelate the disciplines with care but without apology. We will venture into the areas of what in fact is done in *practiced* ministry. Just as the grace of God was not fully known until it became incarnate in Jesus the Christ, so ministry will not be fully known until its incarnation in practice is realized in calls made, counsel given, policy decided, and minutes of meetings written.

A major issue in ministry is the situation where clergy are caught in an unresolved tension between doing what they do not wish (administering a congregation) and not doing enough of what they wish to do (performing individual acts of more "priestly" forms of ministry). This tension is often experienced to such a degree that the minister is ashamed of much that is done in ministry. We will seek to address this tension by listening to the words of the author of II Timothy:

> Try hard to show yourself worthy of God's approval,
> as a labourer
> who need not be ashamed.
>
> (II Tim. 2:15, NEB)

Chapter II

The Administrator as Steward

> In the beginning was the Word. . . . [The Word] was in the beginning with God; all things were made through [the Word], and without [the Word] was not anything made that was made. In [the Word] was life, and the life was the light of [all people]. The light shines in the darkness, and the darkness has not overcome it. (John 1:1–5)

> Peter said, "Lord, are you telling this parable for us or for all?" And the Lord said, "Who then is the faithful and wise steward, whom his master will set over his household . . . ? [Those] to whom much is given, of [them] will much be required; and of [those] to whom [people] commit much they will demand the more." (Luke 12:41–48)

> The master commended the dishonest steward for his prudence; for the [children] of this world are wiser in their own generation than the [children] of light. . . . [Those] who [are] faithful in a very little [are] faithful also in much; and [those] who [are] dishonest in a very little [are] dishonest also in much. . . . No servant can serve two masters. (Luke 16:8–13)

> . . . that you might amend what was defective, and appoint elders in every town as I directed you. . . . For a bishop, as God's steward, must be blameless. (Titus 1:5,7)

Is there a key Biblical concept which represents the essence of ministry through administration? We have already seen the limitations of pastor, apostle, prophet, teacher, and especially priest. The terms "elder," "bishop," and "deacon" all represent critical aspects of ministry through administration, but they are terms that tend to distinguish rather than unify. None of them will serve as a unifying symbolic term descriptive of the essence of such ministry. The term must be overarching, centrally related to the administration of order focused in the body of believers. It must represent the attempt to sustain and maintain the precious gift that God has given in the revelation of Jesus as the Christ. We suggest the term "steward."

Upon reflection, it seems utterly amazing that this term has been so little used in discussions of the doctrine of the church and ministry. It may well be a case of neglect because of assumption. Precisely because it is so central we do not address it. This may be too generous an interpretation. No other Biblical term so encapsulates that sense of derivative responsibility (and respond-ability) which is so crucial in what the church should do with what it has been given. Even the dictionary definition of steward, "the person paid to manage another's estate," correctly focuses on what ministers, both lay and clergy, are expected to be doing in this life. Except for the annual every member canvass, the theological and Biblical richness of the concept is left untouched. Important as "giving" is in the life of the church, it is utterly incorrect to put stewardship into the category of "contribution." Stewardship is fundamentally management. It is management *so that* there is an excess to be contributed! Max Weber's writing on the relation between the Protestant ethic and the spirit of capitalism[35] pointed to this meaning of stewardship, which pervaded the followers of the Reformation. They had a strong sense of responsibility, which made them good managers, which led to prosperity, which provided capital for further investment rather than selfish luxury.

A current theological fashion gives a great deal of currency to the term "co-creator" as descriptive of the general ministry one is expected to perform. That term would cause untold agony in the minds and hearts of the Calvinist Reformers. They could not imagine claiming an equality with the Triune God by whose graciousness our very life has been made possible! God, whose name our Hebrew parents were even hesitant to speak, is the only Creator . . . and Redeemer. The gift of the Spirit is that we might begin to act like stewards and not like God's equals.

Stewardship is not always performed faithfully, as the several New Testament parables on the subject clearly underline. Stewards can act as if the estate belongs to them, or they can seek to bury their treasure for fear that they will make a mistake. They can also be deceitful, dishonest, and downright treacherous. The parables on the misunderstanding of the term "steward" were not meant to eliminate its use, but rather to describe how it might *be used* creatively. About the only place we still use the term is in church structures and agencies that designate boards of stewards or trustees. There are endless tales of trustees who see their first task to be one of "*protecting* investments," or who justify questionable practices such as special privileges, discounts, or kickbacks because they are purchasing services in the name of "the church." Such trustees seem to have taken only part of the stewardship parables to heart without listening to the parables in their wholeness.

We believe that the essence of all ministry is best understood by referring to the minister as first and foremost a faithful steward.

From the Perspective of John's Gospel

The Biblical resources for discussing stewardship are many-sided. One could profitably mine the riches of one or more of the parables in which Jesus expands our understanding of what it means to be a steward (Matthew 25; Mark 12; Luke 16; etc.). One could also approach stewardship through the imagery of bodily unity and use passages from the epistles where such unity is explicated (I Corinthians 12; Ephesians 4; etc.). Or one could point to the pastoral epistles, which indicate that a major function of the bishops is stewardship

(Titus 1:7). Other passages speak of stewardship in describing all Christians (I Cor. 4:1; Gal. 4:2; I Peter 4:10–11). Meaningful as such approaches would be, we will focus instead upon a perspective of stewardship that the Gospel of John provides.

We choose John for several reasons. It is the most symbolic Gospel in seeking to express the paradoxical meanings of all images used in its language. It is the Gospel in which the cosmic dimensions of the revelation in Jesus as the Christ are most forcefully presented. It thereby enlarges our concerns beyond any possible narrow interpretation of stewardship. In John we find a spiritual unity with all of creation: bread is no longer simply bread but becomes the bread of life; water is enriched to include the symbol of living water. Words are transformed from mere linguistic convention to the word of life, and death itself falls before the power of the Christ to grant life. John's audience was not merely the faithful remnant who needed help and sustenance following the death and resurrection of their Lord. John addresses, in addition, all devout and thoughtful persons with his rich material and spiritual imagery. As C. H. Dodd has written:

> Thus the very nature of the symbolism employed by the evangelist reflects his fundamental *Weltanschauung.* He writes in terms of a world in which phenomena—things and events—are a living and moving image of the eternal, and not a veil of illusion to hide it, a world in which the Word is made flesh.[36]

For John the events in time become our access to eternal realities. His Gospel is a "book of signs" giving a special quality of stewardship to our whole cosmic life. In John the blind are made to see and the blindness of the sighted is judged. His is an eschatology that is both now and not yet.

For anyone who doubts the meaning in actions, John presents a unity of word and deed. John would never have accepted any simple distinction between theory and practice, nor would he have approved any move to denigrate "the practical" in ministry. It is no surprise that when H. Richard

Niebuhr sought a Biblical analogue for his Christ the Transformer of Culture (the "conversionist" position) he pointed to the Gospel of John.[37]

We believe this "conversionist" position is consistent with and supportive of the concept of stewardship. The minister as steward, like the conversionist, will have a relatively positive view of creation. As Niebuhr observed, as creatures working in a created world, we live, in the view of the conversionist, "under the rule of Christ and by the creative power and ordering of the divine Word." This causes the conversionist to have an "affirmative and ordered response . . . to the creative, ordering work of God," in spite of the fact that we "may administer perversely the order" given us with our existence.[38] Thus the minister as steward will see positive possibilities in institutions of culture (including the church as institution) which a dualist would not acknowledge. For the dualist, institutions have largely a negative function in this corrupt world.[39]

Again, as Niebuhr observed, history is the story of the mighty deeds of God and our response to them. The conversionist "lives somewhat less 'between the times' and somewhat more in the divine 'Now' than do [dualists]. The conversionist is less concerned with conservation of what has been given in creation, less with preparation for what will be given in final redemption, than with the divine possibility of a present renewal."[40]

These ideas are declared profoundly in the Gospel of John:

> The Fourth Gospel's historical view is characterized by its substitution of the phrase "eternal life" for "kingdom of God." As practically all students of the Gospel have pointed out, that phrase means a quality, a relation to life, a present community through the Spirit with the Father and the Son, a present spiritual worship, love, and integrity.[41]

The steward (consistent with the Johannine message), however, is at the same time not naive about the extent to which conversion has taken place:

> [John] is also on his guard against the confusion of faith with the speciously universal spiritualism of contemporary secular culture. Hence for him the Christian life is cultural life converted by the regeneration of [the human] spirit; but the rebirth of the spirit of all [people] and the transformation of all cultural existence [is] by the incarnate Word.[42]

It is appropriate to remind ourselves of two specific characteristics of the way John organizes his Gospel. On the one hand, he develops the Gospel through a series of episodes in the life of Jesus, each of them with a narrative describing an act or an event, and then a discourse on the meaning of the event. In each case, consistent with the Johannine prologue, the Act and the Word are one. The meaning of the act is not fully understood without the interpretive discourse, and the discourses are not abstract philosophical treatises but are always rooted in an acting and living reality. So too, the minister as steward is not simply to act, for the acts are not complete without interpreting their meanings for self and for others. Likewise, the minister as steward is unfaithful to the model of John's Gospel if that steward believes that ministry is limited to preaching and interpreting without the correlate acts.

A second characteristic of John's Gospel is that he has developed the acts and narratives in relation to the feasts of the religious year as experienced by the Jews. Again, there are tangible acts upon which to build narratives and discourses, but they are *particular* acts. They were the acts of religious people: marriage feasts, the Feast of the Passover, the Feast of Weeks, the Feast of Tabernacles, and burials. John wanted to portray Jesus as acting in some deliberate order rather than out of some serendipitous series of unrelated, transitory happenings. So it is with the minister as steward: major activities are given events around which the steward is expected to exercise leadership by both acting and interpreting. Often in the Gospel of John, the true meaning of the religious feast is not found in the feast itself but in a happening in the street with those gathered for the feast.

While observing the feasts, the Johannine Jesus is constantly enriching, expanding, and challenging the meaning of the religious ritual.

For all of the help we get from John in understanding the full meaning of stewardship—unity of act and interpretation, the cosmic character of Christ's revelation and redemption, a positive view of the possibilities of the "eternal Now," and conversion as a motif for daily life in relation to the rhythm of the religious year—John leaves us with a major concern: what is to be included in our stewardship responsibility and what is to be excluded?

It is easier to answer this question by what John is *not* saying than by what he *is* saying. Certainly, as Niebuhr has pointed out, John is *not* saying that the Christian steward lives with a separatist attitude toward life, for all of life comes under the influence of the Cosmic Christ, *but* there are still some remaining exclusivistic elements in John's Gospel. E. F. Scott commented on this paradox when he said: "The Fourth Gospel, which gives the grandest expression of the universalism of the Christian religion, is . . . at the same time the most exclusive of the New Testament writings."[43] The Gospel of John, therefore, leaves us with a seeming contradiction. While ministers as stewards are not allowed to interpret their task in any narrow or restrictive fashion (therefore being extremely inclusive in outlook), at the same time they stand for a particular interpretation of reality that points to the special character of the revelation in Jesus as the Word (and therefore is exclusive). John is telling us to be stewards of inclusion *and* exclusion.

Inclusion and Exclusion

We are up against one of the most profound problems that has faced the Christian church and its leadership down through the centuries. Are there any boundaries *whatsoever* to the areas of life in which the church should seek to influence or control? Having rejected simple limits that stem from a "two worlds" position, are Christian leaders then left with no alternative but to become victims of megalomania? How does one accept a cosmic notion of stewardship responsibility and still acknowledge a relatively low doctrine of the human?

At the practical level, any person who has lived through the late 1960's and the 1970's knows how hotly this debate has been waged. Christians not only in America but throughout the world have been arguing about where the limits to church influence and action ought to come. In countless local congregations clergy and laity have disputed whether funds should be sent to support certain types of action groups. National denominations have echoed the contest in annual meetings. The World Council of Churches Program to Combat Racism has been defended against critics on the grounds that designated grants should go to radical political liberation movements because the church should "move beyond charity and involve itself in the redistribution of power."[44]

These debates are only recent expressions of issues long at stake in the life of the church. Some have solved the dilemma by establishing theocracies (or to be more precise "clerocracies"). Others, notably Calvinists, have stopped just short of that solution. Calvin, for example, set limits on the areas of life in which the Consistory exercised discipline, leaving other matters to the city councils. Calvin himself did not even accept citizenship and the right to vote in Geneva until an invitation from the magistrates came when he was already fifty years old. He feared the charge of political ambition given the close connections between church and state not only in Geneva but elsewhere in Europe.[45]

John Knox also stopped short of desiring any clerocracy but still strongly maintained the right of the church to speak and act in areas not strictly seen as religious. In developing the *First Book of Discipline,* he assumed some division between church and state when he submitted the book to the Privy Council for approval. The line between the religious and the secular was blurred enough in that document, however, that the Privy Council coldly received and hesitated to approve it. The hesitation was because of the way in which church discipline was related to public vice and because of the provision it contained for public financial support of the reformed churches. Clearly too, in Knox's mind, his insistence on and support for public education under church influence blurred the line demarking limits to Christian stewardship.

Both at the local school and university levels the *First Book of Discipline* provided for full education not only in religion but in grammar, logic, rhetoric, classical and modern languages, and literature.[46] Knox assumed that the care and reformation of religion was one of the primary duties of civil rulers, both high and low.[47] That is further evidence of his blurred line of stewardship and responsibility. His infamous treatise *The First Blast of the Trumpet Against the Monstrous Regiment of Women* gives even more testimony on the point. It shows that in his mind there was no clear distinction between the religious and the secular. Knox strongly opposed clergy control of even the church, much less the state, for of the forty members in the first General Assembly of the reformed Church of Scotland, only six were clergy.

These historical references give considerable support for a stewardship of ministry that is *in*clusive, and they reveal at least some sense of a stewardship of *ex*clusion, but they do not give precise boundary lines as to where the exclusion begins.

In the more contemporary period, Paul Tillich addressed the same dilemma, and he supplied somewhat more precise guidance in the matter. In Part IV of his *Systematic Theology,* when discussing the unity of life,[48] he rejected the use of a metaphor like "level" to interpret the relation between religion and culture, and he suggested instead the metaphor "dimension":

> The replacement of the metaphor "level" by the metaphor "dimension" represents an encounter with reality in which the unity of life is seen above its conflicts. These conflicts are not denied,

> but they are not derived from the hierarchy of levels; they are consequences of the ambiguity of all life processes and are therefore conquerable without the destruction of one level by another. They do not refute the doctrine of the multidimensional unity of life.[49]

The dimensions of life are distinguished from each other on the basis of whether or not certain aspects of life are either actualized or only potential. In the most inclusive dimension of life, the dimension of the spirit, all of the other dimensions are included because they are all actualized. In this dimension of the spirit we find culture, religion, and morality. Under the conditions of existence, Tillich believed that there will never be moral decisions which are not ambiguous:

> There is no straight and certain way to the norms of action in the dimension of the spirit. The sphere of the potential is partly visible, partly hidden. Therefore, the application of a norm to a concrete situation in the realm of the spirit is a venture and a risk. It requires courage and acceptance of the possibility of failure. *The daring character of life in its creative functions holds true also in the dimension of the spirit, in morality, culture, and religion.*[50] (Italics added)

Thus Tillich acknowledged that there are indeed different dimensions to life, and that these will intersect, interact, and come into conflict when moral issues are at stake. He suggested that acting persons will need to accept a degree of risk in their actions. That is the "daring character of life."

While the ambiguity of the unity that underlies the notion of stewardship is not eliminated at any point by Tillich, greater clarity concerning its forms emerges when we consider (among what he called the "constructing" functions of the churches[51]) the relating functions of the churches.[52] Tillich described three ways in which the church as social group relates to other social groupings in the culture: the way of silent interpenetration (priestly), the way of critical judgment (prophetic), and the way of political establishment (royal). In each way, not only does the church have an impact upon the culture, but the culture has an impact upon the churches. All three ways function under the polarity of exclusion and inclusion (or what Tillich called the polarity of opposing and belonging).

As the church has a stewardship responsibility for all of life, it must at the same time not claim to *be* all of life. It must depend primarily upon the first two ways of relating to the other groupings in the culture (the priestly and the prophetic ways), for they are "within the religious sphere,"[53] but it must not ignore the political function. However,

> if the churches act politically, they must do it in the name of the Spiritual Community, i.e., Spiritually. This excludes the use of means which contradict its character as Spiritual Community, such as the use of military force, intoxicating propaganda, and diplomatic ruses, the arousing of religious fanaticism, and so on. The more sharply a church rejects such methods, the more power it will ultimately exercise, for its real power lies in its being a creation of the Spiritual Presence.[54]

Such explication does not bring simple solutions to the ambiguity of stewardship, but it does prevent us from accepting too readily any easy solution concerning the limits of the exercise of stewardship:

> Such phrases as "the church against the world" point to the one principle which essentially determines the relation of the churches to society as a whole and which should determine it actually. Yet if such phrases are used without being balanced by other phrases, such as "the church within the world," they have an arrogant ring and miss the ambiguity of the religious life.[55]

The Coordinating Function

In examining the ways secular administrative disciplines can assist in actualizing the gift of administration, we need first to try to gain some perspective on the stereotypes that so often inform clergy when they are discussing business characteristics and personalities. Why have we reserved some of our most negative opinions for those who function in the realm of capitalistic enterprise? Such a tendency has a curious side when one recognizes how well represented business persons are in the membership of most mainline American Protestant denominations.

As with all stereotypes, such opinions would not continue to exist if there were not some degree of truth in them. At the same time they are distortions of reality. For example, the mass media frequently use stereotypes in portraying both clergy and business leaders. Most clergy bristle at the mealy-mouthed cinematic portrayal of an ineffective minister radiating sweetness and light, but join in the general laughter at the television portrayal of a business mogul whose only concern is profit. Without some reality in the "sweetness and light" clergyperson or the "profit first" business executive, the stereotypical portrayals would cease to function as a tool of the artist. At the same time, such artistic portrayals are not the most appropriate resources for understanding theoretical positions related to either of the professional groups.

There is a sense in which stereotypical exaggeration can be useful. For example, few clergy would deny that business corporations exert great influence on government policies and our common life generally. They would be quick to point out that often this influence is not intentional but is the product of the existence of the corporations as particular social groupings in Western culture. These business groupings silently interpenetrate our whole common life without our even being aware of it, indeed often without the business corporations themselves necessarily having intended the outcomes that do in fact emerge. Meanwhile, the same clergy who can expand this general idea with ease may well be those who are blind to the "priestly" way that the church relates to other social groups, i.e., the "way of silent interpenetration"! In working between ecclesiology and administrative theory we will come to a clearer understanding of churches *simply because* of our frequently negative views of the functioning of business enterprises.

We believe, with Rudge and others, that the "systemic" view of management is the most appropriate management theory to incorporate with church leadership and ministry through administration. Theoreticians and practitioners labeled as systemic cover a wide range of options. In one sense, a systemic view of reality is very old. Any early thinker who viewed creation as orderly, or who had developed a variant on a natural-law theory of creation, was an exponent of the systems school. Only in the twentieth century, however, has this notion most fully begun to influence theorists of management as they have sought to understand and control large human enterprises.[56]

Daniel Wren has suggested four ways in which systems approaches have influenced management and practice: the relations to management theory, the relations to organizations theory, systems analysis and model building, and information systems.[57] Management theory and organizational theory give real attention to integrating management activities both internally and in relation to the organizational and larger human and social environment. Systems analysis and information systems have concentrated much more on the microanalysis of internal operations and the gathering of information from within the particular organization itself. At the same time they acknowledge the importance of information from the social, political, and economic environment.

Contemporary secular management thinking recognizes the interrelated unity of human activity and at the same time seeks practical methods for managing within that unity. The methods developed have been most productive on internal organizational issues. The complexity of the external environment makes full methodological application of a total systems theory much more difficult.

In a serious way contemporary management theory seeks to come to grips with the interrelated character of the total human environment and diligently searches for information on the impact of various actions on our total environment. It is not stretching the point to say that the underlying theory for the practice of total stewardship is emerging more significantly from management thought than it is from the work of contemporary theologians and ethicists.

No doubt sophisticated informational systems can be manipulated by clever managers to the end of selfish maximization of corporate profit, but such use is clearly not inherent in the systemic approach itself. For ministers as stewards to denigrate developments within this field of secular thought and practice is to reveal ignorance and to encourage rejection of the church by thoughtful lay persons familiar with the developments in the field.

Finally, the tension of inclusion and exclusion, which faces the minister as steward and contributes ambiguity to the stewardship function, is the same tension and ambiguity that faces the systemic management theorist and practitioner. How much can be included within one's system of thought, and how much must of necessity be excluded? Tillich suggested that the "against the world" position was necessary for the church, but that it had to be balanced by an inclusive "within the world" orientation to avoid arrogance. One can almost reverse the priority when one examines secular systemic thought and methods. They stress the inclusive pole of the tension but need to balance it with an "exclusive" limiting of the system to avoid the pretense of omniscience and omnipotence.

When the insights of the systemic school are placed alongside and in support of the theology of the minister as steward, is it possible to summarize the relationship through one of the traditional management functions?

We believe that "coordination" is the appropriate function to use. The minister as steward seeks to coordinate both internal and external resources for the purposes which the community of believers wishes to accomplish. In such coordination the minister cannot ignore the fact that all actions have counter reactions, both internally and externally. The minister as steward will communicate to the company of believers both by action and words the sense of the interdependent unity in which we all live.

Chapter III

The Administrator as Elder

Do not suppose that I have come to abolish the Law and the prophets; I did not come to abolish, but to complete. . . . If any . . . therefore [set] aside even the least of the Law's demands, and [teach] others to do the same, [they] will have the lowest place in the kingdom of Heaven, whereas [any] who [keep] the Law, and [teach] others so, will stand high in the kingdom of Heaven. I tell you, unless you show yourselves far better . . . than the Pharisees and the doctors of the law, you can never enter the kingdom of Heaven. (Matt. 5:17–20, NEB)

My intention in leaving you behind in Crete was that you should set in order what was left over, and in particular should institute elders in each town. In doing so, observe the tests I prescribed. (Titus 1:5, NEB)

And now I appeal to the elders of your community, as a fellow-elder and a witness of Christ's sufferings, and also a partaker in the splendour that is to be revealed. Tend that flock of God whose shepherds you are, and do it, not under compulsion, but of your own free will, as God would have it; not for gain but out of sheer devotion; not tyrannizing over those who have been allotted to your care, but setting an example to the flock. (I Peter 5:1–3, NEB)

They also appointed elders for them in each congregation, and with prayer and fasting committed them to the Lord in whom they had put their faith. (Acts 14:23, NEB)

Shared Leadership

Ministry is often perceived as a lonely profession. The image which readily comes to mind as we think about the leadership of local congregations is that of isolated individuals who are responsible for the life of their parishioners. These persons set the schedule of worship, write and deliver the sermons, visit the sick, minister to the needy, and generally go about doing good in the community.

This image of the leader functioning alone seems to inform some of the self-selectivity of those who choose to enter this profession. Ministers are not known for their ability to function in teams, and how seldom professional church staffs function harmoniously for more than a short time. There are many complex reasons behind the fact that the norm of American Protestant church life is the single (functioning alone) ordained clergyperson ministering to a local congregation. One of the reasons undoubtedly is that most clergy prefer to work alone. They may, with some regularity, bemoan the fact that there is so much to be done, and they could certainly profitably use assistance and support. Nevertheless, they know that they actually prefer the freedom that one-person leadership provides.

In spite of numerous attempts to form clergy associations and professional groups within American Protestantism, these have never developed the strength that one finds in other professions. They are relatively ineffective. The Protestant ministry not only appears to be a lonely profession, but it will likely remain so.

In the face of this situation, it is strange how little formal attention is given to the matter of the role, function, and nature of lay leaders within local congregations. While all major denominational polities have provision for the election or appointment of a variety of types of lay leaders at the congregational level, rarely do seminary curricula require a course in the "Theology and Function of Lay Leadership." We give lip service to the central place that lay leaders occupy in the life of Christian churches, but we do not often discuss how to develop and work with lay leaders in the congregation.

In this chapter we propose to examine this issue as it relates to the gift of administration. Specifically, we want to look at that level of lay leadership that is elected or appointed to share with the professional leader in making policy and planning the work of the congregation. Our focus is on leaders who perform the same function as a board of directors or trustees of a corporation or a school.

When lay leadership is discussed in a church context, the discussion is usually of how a voluntary institution performs its task in the absence of enough paid professionals. Our concern is with those functions which need to be performed in *any* social grouping, whether or not it has sufficient resources to employ persons to do the actual work of that association. We will address the issue of shared leadership, which is present in congregational ministry whether there is only one, or more than one, person employed to perform leadership functions. This is the function that the Judeo-Christian heritage has traditionally recognized as belonging to the "elders."

The Tradition of Elders

In the Christian church the use of elders is a tradition carried over from Judaism, modified to fit Christian needs. In the Old Testament, elders performed several functions: they were leaders in war, they were judges in disputes (as interpreters of the Law), they were givers of wise advice, and they were witnesses in administration.[58] The use that the early Christian church made of elders is open to considerable debate and multiple interpretations. It is therefore useful to turn to the work of Hans von Campenhausen for a review of the role of elders.[59]

Von Campenhausen's work on elders was set within the larger framework of his study of ecclesiastical authority and office in the first three centuries. His summary thesis was that "the abiding presuppositions of the whole succeeding development of office in the Church and of its spiritual authority" were fashioned in antiquity.[60] His overall argument on all of the various offices was set up as a tension between "office organised on a legal basis and free spiritual authority."[61] While the perfect combination of official and charismatic authority is found only once, in Jesus himself, in Von Campenhausen's view, the best that the church can attain is to subordinate both office and charisma to Christ as the Living Word rather than to choose either "authoritarian" or "enthusiast" distortions of the concept of leadership in the church. His argument was that the "apostles" stood in a second-generation relation to Jesus' authority and spiritual power. They themselves were not individually important but they turned over the power and authority to the church. Then in a third generation of leadership the *interplay* between the two poles of office and charisma developed.

Paul's writings tend to support the free charismatic forms of leadership. In Von Campenhausen's view, Paul develops a theological rationale for this emphasis that is better than his appreciation for the sociological consequences. Alongside the Pauline developments, the Jewish Christians developed the church led by elders. As Von Campenhausen has written:

> Here (among Jewish Christians) from the very first the "elders," even where their rights are understood in purely patriarchal terms, possess "official" authority, that is to say authority based on their position. The legal order is combined with the "natural" order of age, experience, and personal ascendency, and now tends, in a way quite alien to Paul, to enhance within the Church, as it does so often, the moral importance of natural human attributes. Nevertheless, office is thought of as by definition spiritual. For it leads the Christian congregation, which is a spiritual community; and consequently the office too is spiritual in its origin and in its goals, and must be spiritual in the manner in which it is carried out.[62]

Von Campenhausen saw the tension between the Pauline charismatic freedom and the "official" thinking of the pastoral epistles being held together somewhat in Luke and I Peter. But the church in the early centuries, and indeed in later centuries as well, tended to choose the pole of office rather than the pole of charismatic freedom. This tendency came to its ultimate conclusion in the doctrine of penance and in the declaration that the bishop of Rome had ultimate, preeminent authority. Von Campenhausen believed this development to be partially explained as follows. The early Christian church faced an opposite problem from that presented to Paul. Paul had to struggle against the exaggerated Jewish "law," while later Christians had to struggle against the confusion and proliferation of competing enthusiastic sects. Von Campenhausen's ultimate answer was to have both office *and* charisma subservient to Jesus as the Christ and to give attention to the *whole* Biblical testimony without choosing the emphases of either the Pauline or the pastoral epistles.

The reason for examining the specific contribution of the office of elder is to understand its positive roots and to assist the ordained clergy to see themselves as elders working with other elders on the policies and plans of the church. We believe this will assist clergy in addressing the tension between office and charisma. It reduces the expectation that they must in their own person possess all the gifts and perform all the offices. What then were the functions of the elders in the early church?

The early church did not slavishly adopt the notion of elder from Jewish practices. While indeed there was still the relation of the elders to the law, the relation was not to the old Jewish law but to the new and living law which fulfilled the intent of the old. In addition, the new church had its own traditions to nurture and safeguard. Thus the elders had the responsibility of being "guardians" of the teaching of the church against false teachings and heresies. Even Paul saw the need for this guardianship function. In his farewell to the

Ephesian elders he admonished them by saying, "Keep watch over yourselves and over all the flock of which the Holy Spirit has given you charge, as shepherds of the church of the Lord, which he won for himself by his own blood" (Acts 20:28, NEB). By this definition the first function of the elder is a conserving one. It is focused on protecting the tradition against inappropriate revisions or modifications. This function by itself can lead to authoritarianism, as the church was to discover in its early history.

The concept of elder, however, includes a second function: that of setting a human example or model. Frequently the pastoral epistles emphasize this second function. In such an emphasis, the place of "natural" leaders is recognized. Elders are to be persons who by their natural endowments of age, experience, general moral uprightness, and community respect are fit to be called by the term. Clearly the appeal here is to consider natural human qualifications in selecting leaders. While this can be seen as an appeal in opposition to a more spiritual standard, such an interpretation is not necessary. Von Campenhausen put it this way:

> Even the new authority of the "elders," acquired by human appointment, should not be thought of as in essence "human," nor as such is it bound without question to prove "legalistic." The only relevant consideration is the way in which it is thought of in practice and explained in principle. It is not unspiritual just so long as it remains obedient to the Spirit of Christ, and performs that service of the Gospel of Christ for which it was appointed. Only where this original evangelical relation is inverted, and the authority of the official made absolute, is the primitive Christian concept of the church abandoned; and at first this question nowhere arises.[63]

This second aspect of the role of elders, setting a human example, by itself could distort the role of elder by becoming "moralistic" or "patriarchal." To point inordinately to the human "uprightness" of the elder would overemphasize the moral element, and to point excessively to the age or wisdom of the elder would be to develop a patriarchate. Either could miss the new life in the spirit which the gospel of Jesus Christ called forth.

As the church moved through the first three centuries the *office* of elder developed as a "third generation" phenomenon. Elders were no longer simply persons of advanced years and wisdom; they were congregationally recognized persons responsible for guarding the tradition and possessing certain human qualities of leadership. Adopting such an office did not undermine the principle of the independent authority of the congregation as a whole guarding the tradition. The congregation was the place where the recognition of eldership was bestowed.

We argued that the Gospel of John with its cosmic concerns provided an appropriate backdrop for the study of responsible stewardship. In considering the *purpose* of elders, the appropriate reference is the Gospel of Matthew. This may seem unusual since the Gospel of Luke contains the most frequent reference to elders. Our concern is to examine that Gospel writer who most helpfully addresses the appropriate use of tradition and at the same time speaks most about the moral implications of the Christian life. Maintaining the tradition and human moral modeling were the primary functions that the elder fulfilled.

Matthew best addresses these two concerns even though he does not speak of elders in any formal or direct sense. Floyd Filson in writing a commentary on Matthew[64] pointed to some features of the Gospel which make it an appropriate one for elders:

> [Matthew] was a Christian teacher, who wrote what he had been teaching, and arranged it to enable others to share effectively in this continual teaching task. The Church, which emerged within Judaism and yet soon spread beyond the bounds of Judaism, needed an interpretation of the O.T. which would be faithful to its historical roots and yet would give Christians a vivid sense of the miraculous new work of God in Jesus Christ. It needed clues to the deep meanings of God's work in this historical figure. . . . It needed some clues as to how grace and discipline are to

> be combined in the community life of disciples.[65] . . . [Matthew's] intense concern for the relation between the Jewish Law and the Christian gospel, and the note of controversy with Jewish sects, indicate that he was a Jewish Christian. . . . His deep Jewish roots and loyalty are combined with catholic contacts and outlook.[66]

In Matthew's five great discourses of Jesus we see some paralleling of the use of Mosaic law in Judaism. As Filson argued, to a great extent Jesus had a positive attitude toward the Mosaic law and meant to fulfill its intent.[67] When the teaching of the Pharisees is consistent with the Law they are to be listened to even if their *practices* are to be ignored and rejected. "The main drive of Jesus' teaching in Matt. is clear; he rejects the oral tradition, and does so to protect the importance and authority of the Law contained in Scripture."[68] Matthew saw Jesus as the Royal Messiah who fulfills both the Law and the Prophets.

Elders in the early church fulfilled the "third generational" need for continuity. Also, they represented an early example of the importance of natural gifts in the selection of leaders. While there is only marginal evidence concerning exact ways in which elders functioned, what evidence there is indicates that they were very widely used. They appear also to be persons who form a group within local congregations. While not all elders are considered bishops, all bishops appear to have been elders. The review indicates that the use of offices, and particularly the office of elder, was not a late addition to congregational practice but was present in the very early centuries.

Over the intervening centuries, most of the themes outlined have been developed within the various denominational polity patterns. Elders, whether or not formally called by that title, have been variously regarded. In some traditions they have been seen as one of the clergy categories; in other traditions they have been seen as lay congregational leaders. Ruling and teaching elders have been distinguished in some traditions. Some have seen the elder role as one step in an ordination sequence, and still others have seen it as a terminal election. In some traditions the office has been for a set period of time, while in others it is a lifetime appointment subject only to processes of discharge for inappropriate functioning and behavior. What is relatively constant in all of these various traditions of the office is the concern for the maintenance of valid teaching and some concern for "natural" attributes being incorporated (along with knowledge of the tradition) into the selection of persons for the office.

This review underlines the importance of the role of elder in the gift of administration, and it demonstrates that the use of such an office does not stand in opposition to New Testament charismatic and spiritual emphases. The role of elder may indeed become distorted, by inordinate emphasis on only part of its definition, but the early church recognized and addressed such a distortion. We turn now to a consideration of the theological tension under which the office functions.

Equality and Competition

Sociologically the church shares one concern with every other institution: the perpetuation of the purpose and tradition for which it was founded. The early church addressed that concern by the appointment of elders. By definition, these persons have a "conservative" function and are normally appointed to oversee maintenance, not to stimulate innovation.

Previously, we have discussed one type of theological tension under which these elders function, namely, the tension of office and charismatic gift. That tension, however, is shared with all the offices we are examining and which we incorporate in the phrase "gift of administration." However, any group of leaders faces another theological tension: Paul Tillich described it as the "ambiguity of competition and equality."[69]

In every social group Tillich saw a pattern of continuous,

dynamic decision-making. The pattern is one of continuous encounter and conflict. Such encounter is the very essence of social life:

> There is a pushing ahead in all these encounters, a trying, a withdrawing into an existing unity, a pushing out of it, a coalescing, a splitting, a continuous alternation between victory and defeat.[70]

In principle all elders are equal, but in practical competition with each other (both in terms of their interpretation of what *is* the valid definition of the tradition and in terms of their individual natural attributes) an inequality always emerges. This pattern is further complicated in that the tradition is, finally, the possession of the whole church and not just the elders. Therefore, elders are in competition with general opinions in the church as well as in competition among themselves. Some see this constant conflict in the midst of fundamental equality and presumed harmony to be antithetical to Christian life. There should be agreement, some would say, about the content of the Christian tradition. They would see lack of agreement as evidence of a lack of faith. We believe, on the contrary, that such conflict is not only inevitable; it is in fact a sign of *life* in the group.

The New Testament writers and the early church fathers who wrote about elders intended that the office should prevent the growth of heresy and the proliferation of Christian sects. Elders were appointed for that reason. The early writers recognized, however, that the elders would disagree among themselves and that the congregation might from time to time have to remove them from their office. These early theologians were, perhaps unconsciously, working from a theory of democratic decision-making, always under the influence of the Holy Spirit. It is not clear whether elders made decisions by consensus, by majority vote, by "significant" majorities, or by some other process. It is clear, however, that they *were* in disagreement with each other on various issues. Thus the office of elder does not eliminate the ambiguity of equality and competition; rather, it becomes a means for the maintenance of valid tradition and the search for right purposes within the Christian community.

In considering the issue of competition among elders within their fundamental equality, one wonders how often certain points of view "won the day" on the basis of theological argument and an appeal to the Christian tradition and how often persons won arguments on the basis of their outstanding moral character and natural leadership abilities. In all probability the early church had as much difficulty sorting out that mix of personality and rationality as we do.

Conserving the Heritage

In the contemporary American scene, a single (functioning alone) ordained minister works with a board or council of congregationally elected "elders" who share with the minister the responsibility for general oversight of congregational life. We limit our comments below to those situations in which the single ordained minister is dealing with those "elders" (or lay leaders) who function in relation to overall general policy matters.

Consistent with the historical background already outlined, we are considering that the ordained clergy are, themselves, elders. They share responsibility for the maintenance of the tradition and they have been appointed with consideration given to their "natural" leadership attributes. Likewise, we assume that elders, as elders, rarely function alone but form a group that makes decisions and approves policies. Eldership is by historical definition a team enterprise.

Clergy frequently express concern that boards of elders are too conservative and not sufficiently risk oriented. The implication is that boards of elders are difficult groups with which to work. This complaint is more easily understood by reference to dominant American cultural values than by reference to Christian tradition. As Americans we put a great deal of value on innovation and creativity. What is of value is that which is new. As we have seen, however, the function of elders is to test any new interpretation or idea to see if it is consistent with the tradition. Therefore, not only does one expect elders to be conservative, but one would be most worried if they were the "innovative" body in the church! Elders should be presented with innovative interpretations of traditional beliefs and practices, but the expectation ought to be that they will put such ideas to rigorous test. They will need to be convinced. A real concern would emerge when elders are prepared to accept almost any proposal without discussion and questioning. In such a situation one would doubt that they truly understood the function they were appointed to perform.

Another concern that clergy express about elders is that they are too "building and materials oriented" and not sufficiently "people oriented." This is a more complex problem. One relatively simple question to ask is whether the right issues are being presented to the elders for discussion. On the face of it, buildings and materials issues are only tangentially related to the maintenance of tradition. Once the policies of program have been discussed and approved, the details for carrying them out are properly assigned elsewhere in the congregational structure.

People and programs are not disembodied from physical realities. Therefore, material concerns may quite properly be considered when making policy decisions. Also, buildings frequently take on theological significance and become a way in which human beings identify with certain fundamental "meanings." Thus clergy as elders working with fellow elders will examine with some care the charge that elders appear to be "building and not people oriented." Are issues being presented to the elders in appropriate ways? Is the organizational structure of the congregation sufficiently differentiated? Can the congregation be encouraged to focus on the "meanings" in buildings rather than the buildings themselves?

Frequently the objection to elders is raised that they do not "know the Christian tradition," so they cannot be expected to function appropriately. Combined with this complaint is the lament that they were appointed or elected because they were successful leaders in business or other secular organizations and not because they were informed Christians. Again, on the face of it, it is easy to be sympathetic with such objections, but they need to be looked at with some care. In the first place, "natural" attributes of leadership, even in the earliest Christian centuries, were regarded as important in the selection of elders. To have achieved community recognition of leadership ability is hardly a disqualifying condition for being an elder. Some clergy may not like "real leaders" to be among the elders since they cannot easily manipulate them into particular types of decision-making. The clergy might ask themselves whether the nominating body did not have real insight in insisting that such persons be appointed as elders!

But, on the more substantive issue of lacking knowledge of the Christian heritage, other responses need to be made. Are the elders lacking in Christian understanding or do they just not share the biases of the clergy? If they are truly lacking, how adequate is the adult education program of the church? How creative is the program of orientation for eldership? Has the church developed any continuing educational program for officers? Do the clergy think they have to do all of this education alone or are they taking advantage of opportunities for the elders which exist already or could be developed outside the local congregation? Ministry through administration means working on answers to these questions. It does not mean simple "paperwork."

Finally, some would see the elders as being too contentious among themselves or in relation to clergy. Again, this is not, according to the historical background, a necessary symbol of failure but a possible symbol of *life* within the group.

We turn now to a consideration of the insights from the administrative disciplines that can assist in the understanding of eldership.

Organizing and Planning

We have emphasized how the role of elder is related to maintaining the tradition and thus have placed the eldership role in a conservative focus. This is an entirely appropriate emphasis, but it partially obscures the way in which the minister engages with other elders in leading the church into fulfilling its mission. In order to clarify the working relationships among elders it is necessary to turn to the administrative disciplines and consider some of the functions that are associated with management of any group activity.

Management theorists only roughly agree concerning the number, names, and descriptions of various management functions. Daniel A. Wren[71] compared nine theorists and found that they named anywhere from three to seven major administrative functions. They used twelve different titles to identify the functions, and there was not common agreement concerning which functions were subcategories and which were major categories. In fact, there were only two functions which all of the authors named as major: planning and organizing. One of these, planning, relates directly to the role of elder.

It may seem at first glance to be paradoxical to suggest that a function like planning, which is oriented to the future, is the function most directly related to the elder's role of maintaining tradition. However, it is precisely in the process of "designing the future" that organizational purpose and the maintenance of tradition are most appropriately addressed.

Imagine two different congregations engaged in annual meetings where the leaders are reviewing activities and accomplishments of the past year. In one congregation, the "elders" had done little conscious planning for the year. Consequently they are in no position to evaluate activities and projects undertaken. The assumption behind such a style of leadership is that the organization is doing the right thing and simply should continue to function as before.

Such a review is a prescription for disaster. There is no basis for knowing what, of the many things which took place, should be reported. There is no basis for knowing which elements of the report should be stressed in detail and which should be treated superficially. There is no conscious awareness of which issues are tense ones within the group and which ones are of no basic interest whatsoever. People can discuss reports therefore only in idiosyncratic terms. Such discussions become a basis for raising private interpretations of the purpose of the congregation. They easily deteriorate into discussions of incompetence or irresponsibility. Little can be done concerning the issues except to blame certain persons for the failures which happen to be highlighted by those present.

On the other hand, in the second imagined congregation, the elders and the minister had previously devoted themselves to the function of planning. The plans developed were available for discussion, and the elders agreed with their validity. Among the elders, and in subsequent sharing with the congregation, the minister created an opportunity for discovering the various interpretations of the Christian tradition present in that body of believers. The proposed emphases for program could be shared and responsibilities assigned to various leaders and leadership groups. Then at the time of annual review there is a basis for knowing what issues and programs should be stressed in reports, in terms either of accomplishment or lack of it; and there is a basis for knowing what measures of evaluation should be employed. There is opportunity to focus discussion on other than idiosyncratic concerns.

One wonders why churches so seldom employ planning in significant and meaningful ways. Were it only in churches that the lack of planning is to be noted, one could search for peculiar characteristics of churches that contribute to the omission. However, management theorists generally agree that leaders of various types of organizations not only overlook planning but also fail to recognize it as *the foundation* for all management activity. Without planning, there can be no evaluation. Without planning, organization is haphazard and controlling is without basis. Planning is a necessary but not sufficient basis for effective administration. One may find administrators who plan but are not effective, but one will not find effective administrators who do not plan.

Since leaders of any social enterprise must learn the necessity of planning, one wonders why leaders of Christian organizations so often resist it. An argument could be made that Christianity has a form of resistance to planning that is deeply embedded at the theological/theoretical level. Such an argument would seek to show that all human action is dependent action, that history is the province of God, and that human beings are expected to read meaning into events after the fact rather than seek to influence the future. Such an argument would very likely give major attention to the free moving of God's Spirit in life. Human beings should not inhibit the Spirit by attempting to foreclose future change and novelty of action. It is their place to be ready in freedom to respond to God's actions, and they should not seek to "play God" by outlining future events. This argument can be put in sophisticated forms or it can be the simple resistance of church elders to stewardship campaigns and planned local church budgets. While these same elders probably engage in serious planning efforts in local businesses where they are controlling partners, somehow they believe that within the church context resistance to planning is a symbol of deep "faith."

The minister as elder has the theological task of dislodging such interpretations of Christianity. This involves explaining the dialectical tensions of freedom and order, justification and sanctification, faith and love within the Christian tradition. The grounds for planning would not be successful business practices but the nature of human responsibility, which results from having received the free gift of grace through God's action. Planning as such *facilitates* rather than inhibits one's ability to respond to new developments and changes. The minister can outline how mutual planning is a loving response to the worth of the other person. It permits people to address and resolve differences of opinion. A lack of planning is often an effort to avoid responsibility or to keep other persons "at a distance."

Types of Plans

Ministers as elders will be related to the planning function in a variety of ways depending on the type of plan that is being considered. Harold Koontz and Cyril O'Donnell, in writing on the planning function of management, developed a hierarchy of plans which illustrates the multiple relationships that elders can have to planning.[72] At the top of the pyramid are the "purposes" or "missions" representing the most basic statements of the reason for existence behind the group. From the purposes or missions emerge the objectives. The objectives are broken down into strategies, the strategies are related to the programs that carry out the strategies, and finally the programs are related to the budgets that support them. Policies, procedures, and rules support the strategies, programs, and budgets that Koontz and O'Donnell also list as a part of their hierarchy of types of plans. The higher up the pyramid the type of plan is, the more concern elders would have with the plan.

The basic assumption behind this way of viewing the various types of plans is that planning has a deductive or derivative character to it. Each level of planning should govern the basic content of the plans in the level just below it. This hierarchy seeks to protect the planner from too quickly developing programs and budgets which may reflect the practical realities within which the group must function but which may *not* have examined the principled restrictions of purposes and objectives that should be related to the programs and budgets. In working with such a hierarchical concept of planning, movement from any level in the pyramid to any lower level involves decisions and choices. Several kinds of objectives can fulfill a purpose or mission statement, there is more than one strategy for carrying out objectives, and one can develop several budgets related to a single type of program. The intervening policies, procedures, and rules are developed to assist in clarifying these decisions.

A council of elders would be most concerned with the development of the purpose and mission statement of a church. They might well assist in developing the major objectives that the church will use in any particular time to realize the purposes. They might even exercise oversight of the policies and procedures that groups within the congregation develop relative to the strategies and programs. They would not, however, normally be involved directly (as elders) in the implementation of the strategies, programs, and budgets designed to fulfill the purposes and objectives. They would have a major interest in the review and evaluation that are undertaken following the agreed-upon period of execution.

This brief outline indicates several ways in which planning relates to the eldership function of maintaining and overseeing tradition. Often this ordering of priority is reversed in the actual functioning of elders within a congregation. Instead of focusing their concerns at the top of the pyramid, they focus mainly on the "lowest" level of planning, namely, the budget, and the whole process is short-circuited. Purpose, mission, and objectives are either assumed (and therefore not open to competitive discourse and decision-making) or they are ignored (and therefore lost or changed over time without anyone being conscious that this is happening).

Our intent in relating the planning function of management closely to the role of elder is to stress that priority should be given by elders to the planning of purposes, mission, and objectives. Why is planning so often ineffective at this level?

Inhibitions to Planning by Elders

Since churches are fundamentally voluntary associations, the factors which inhibit planning are of a somewhat different character than those which inhibit planning in other types of organizations. The minister as elder working with other elders needs to address those inhibitions lest serious planning fail before it has even begun. The following list of inhibitions is not exhaustive, but it includes samples of several of the more common factors that undercut planning efforts.

General Lack of Commitment to the Process. Leaders of voluntary associations are commonly appointed or elected with informal assumptions on the part of all concerned that the position will not demand a great deal of time or effort. Elders in churches are no exception. Persons being nominated often indicate a lack of time, knowledge, or ability for the position; the nominator responds that very little is required to fulfill the position. A reluctant candidate results from such a process. The veiled hope of the nominator is that, once in office, the candidate will become dedicated to the position. The serious and complicated work of planning is difficult with a group of such persons.

A minister who expects to take planning with elders seriously would be well advised to outline in advance the expected responsibilities and related time commitments without any hesitation. More often than not, such honesty will evoke deeper interest from the candidates rather than refusal to serve. The hours devoted to the nomination process pay enormous dividends later!

A general lack of commitment to planning can also be related to the "state of health" of the congregation. If its members judge a congregation to be in difficulty, they hesitate to join in planning for the future. They fear predictable failure or the task of simply spelling out an endless list of insolvable problems. At the opposite extreme, in the congregation that appears to be stable or even shows some degree of growth and creativity, people question why the lengthy and difficult planning task is necessary. Strangely enough, both of these objections assume that the present *is* the future. While no simple methods will easily change such "moods" which resist planning, the minister faced with a declining situation will need first to outline for the council of elders ways in which alternative scenarios could affect the future. The minister in the seemingly stable or growing situation will likewise need to portray ways in which leadership decisions can produce change in a variety of directions.

Difficulty in Definition of Objectives. At first glance, the purposes of churches appear peculiarly subject to meaningless generalizations or to unverifiable objectives. H. Richard Niebuhr's definition of the purpose of the church as "the increase of the love of God and neighbor"[73] seems at once to be both general and at the same time unverifiable in any normal sense. Closer examination reveals that it is not as general as it appears. A church adopting such a major planning statement would know that it could not settle for concern only for the love of God *or* only for the love of neighbor. Ultimately objectives and programs would relate to both concerns. Nor could it be satisfied with a situation in which such love was not *increasing.*

Niebuhr's statement is also not completely lacking in means of verification. Clergy and laity alike are constantly applying some form of measurement to how the love of God or neighbor is increased. Little agreement may exist concerning what those measurements are, but all of us apply them most of the time. Some would measure increasing love of God by more attendance at worship, while others would favor particular patterns of worship. Some would measure love of neighbor in terms of particular acts of personal charity; others would relate it to corporate giving patterns or efforts on behalf of certain forms of legislation.

While defining objectives is subject to wide interpretation among Christians, all concerned persons are constantly developing particular forms of verifiable measurement. Keeping such definitions private not only inhibits possible common enrichment through adoption of common objectives, it also sets the stage for bitterness and unproductive disagreement when review and evaluation is attempted.

The struggle for ever more precise definitions of objectives for a congregation and serious discussion of the ways in which meeting those objectives will be measured is effort well expended by a council of elders. We must not be seduced by the argument that defining objectives for churches is impossible and therefore should not be attempted. Even corporations dedicated to making a profit have discovered that profit can be made in a great many ways. It is no simple matter to decide which ways are most consistent with the other, less tangible objectives such as community welfare, public support, and regional growth.

The Problems of Equality and Competition. Our argument has been that elders are both equal and competitive in their function of maintaining tradition. Establishing equality within a heterogeneous group—where some are trained, some not; some paid, some not; some experienced, some not—is not an easy task. Competition between alternative interpretations of the tradition can be kept productive rather than destructive only through the exercise of the greatest care and sensitivity. Self-conscious planning efforts assist this process greatly. Such efforts bring differences in interpretation to everyone's attention before any acts have been committed and while debate and compromise can still be productive.

The advantages of utilizing planning to establish equality and promote productive competition among elders is so obvious, one wonders why local congregations so seldom employ it with vigor. The reasons appear to be other than rational, and therefore more difficult to address. It is a hypothesis worth examining that trained clergy in the final analysis do not believe that lay elders *are* in fact equal to them in ability to interpret the tradition. Seminaries, we fear, contribute to the development of this clergy egotism. Therefore it is not appropriate truly to share equally in the development of the purposes, mission, and objectives of the total work of the local church. Furthermore, working through the difficult competitive debates "before the fact" is a painful process. Clergy are tempted to avoid such pain in the hope that if they develop programs on their own without such debates the program will be so self-evident in its appropriateness and quality that no "after the fact" debate will occur. This type of thinking, while appealing to many of us who are clergy, is either the result of egotism or a product of defining the ordained clergy role as prophet and priest, rather than steward and elder.

Such egotism is fed by numerous laity who are only too willing to defer to the clergy's opinions, at least until trouble occurs. They do this because they do not have an "office" view of ministry and do not fully accept the doctrine of the priesthood of all believers. Possibly they are as eager as the clergy to avoid painful discussions and difficult planning sessions and prefer to "hope for the best." Such laity are also too willing to join in the "blaming" process focused upon the clergy if and when difficulties do emerge.

The Difficulties of Premising and the Unpredictabilities of the Future. One cannot plan without making assumptions concerning the future. Planning inevitably involves "premising,"[74] the effort to construct propositions about future reality. This development of premises combines the roles of steward and elder. It is an effort to predict future developments both within and outside of the congregation; to distinguish those factors over which the congregation has control from those beyond its control; and to discern which future events are likely to produce "problems" in realizing the church's purposes and which events present special opportunities not to be missed. Premising normally involves reviewing at least the recent history of the group, establishing relatively reliable trend lines, gathering external data, and making "educated guesses." It is a time-consuming process and difficult to know when to stop. Simple extrapolations of past trends into the future are rarely reliable. They ignore the hard choices of separating out what is within the capacity of the group to influence from what is not.

Anyone who has ever worked with a group of elders in this process can cite "self studies" that were accurate and helpful in analysis, but hopelessly lacking in prescriptions. Illustrations also abound of churches that in planning could not negotiate between the Scylla of uncontrollable defeat and the Charybdis of unrealizable hopes.

More than one person with resolve to plan has given up the effort after one or two attempts. For all such problems in planning two responses are appropriate: (1) the alternative of no planning is even *more* fraught with unforeseen difficulties where one lacks any capacity to resolve confusion and disagreements, and (2) the planning process, in spite of its obvious troublesome character, builds community, clarifies "hidden agenda" among the elders, raises expectations, focuses responsibilities, and forms the basis for evaluation and team effort.

Flexibility and Planning. Closely linked with the difficulties of premising is the inhibition people feel when faced with a plan that needs changing. Often the person who resists planning is the same one who upon achieving a plan treats it as an inflexible law. Given human finitude, it would be a strange plan indeed which was fulfilled in all detail as time moved along.

Plans are a means to an end and not an end in themselves. They are made to be changed. They are intended to facilitate debate within the life of the congregation. They are intended to clarify purposes and mission and to establish major objectives in the life of the congregation. They are to be utilized as a "tool for ongoing debate." They are nothing less or more than an aid in corporate decision-making. Plans are intended to narrow the range of uncertainty in the common life of the group. They are not intended to eliminate change and adjustment. Serious elders work on plans as though they were intended to be permanent, and, when once developed, treat them as though they were elastic. We will say more about this in the next chapter.

Making Decisions Together

We began this chapter by spelling out the issue of shared leadership which faces the minister functioning within the church as a voluntary association. We close the chapter now by examining some special aspects of the elder's concern for policy, especially the place of policy in a voluntary association.

Management authors frequently affirm that policy formation is the special function of Chief Executive Officers (CEO's). Their position on this matter reflects assumptions concerning a fundamentally hierarchical organization, which is frequent in the business sector of our society. While there are many similarities between business executives and elected or appointed leaders in voluntary associations, there are also important differences. In many respects, clergy functioning as ministers of local congregations or as executive secretaries of church boards or as seminary administrators are in positions similar to company CEO's, but in many ways they are also in quite different positions.

Both business CEO's and church leaders find themselves in central leadership positions.[75] Both kinds of leaders need to have a "generalist" view of the organization rather than a "specialist" view. Nothing in the organization is outside their range of concern. Writers on business management frequently note how difficult it is to move a staff specialist into centralized management. The motivations, satisfactions, and competencies expected of the two types of roles seem to be in conflict. The fact that clergy are trained for the most part by seminary teachers who are specialists rather than generalists makes this difficulty more apparent. A seminary may be compared to a program for CEO's taught by people with only "staff" experience and competence.

CEO's and clergy leaders both need clarified policy within which to function. The policies of profit organizations, however, quickly emerge as different when compared with policies in the not-for-profit organizations. The basic purposes of the not-for-profit organizations are more subject to ambiguity, they often lack consensus, success in meeting objectives is more difficult to quantify, decision-making is normally much more group dominated, and consequently lines of authority and responsibility are more diffuse and blurred. These differences do not eliminate the need to develop policies and plans; they only emphasize that the development of policies and plans in not-for-profit organizations is both more crucial *and* more difficult than in profit institutions.

Given this necessity and this difficulty, wise ministers will utilize to the fullest the resource of the council of elders which they have available in the tradition of the church. The elders do not become a conservative roadblock for the minister, standing in the way of progress. Rather, they are the necessary resource for developing common policies, plans, and major objectives that will enable the church to be a faithful instrument of the purposes of God and not a private enclave for furthering the minister's own interpretation of the gospel.

Chapter IV

The Administrator as Bishop

Jesus was walking by the Sea of Galilee when he saw Simon and his brother Andrew on the lake at work with a casting-net; for they were [fishers]. Jesus said to them, "Come with me, and I will make you fishers of [people]." And at once they left their nets and followed him. (Mark 1:16–18, NEB)

Keep watch over yourselves and over all the flock of which the Holy Spirit has given you charge, as shepherds of the church of the Lord, which he won for himself by his own blood. (Acts 20:28, NEB)

Do not neglect the spiritual endowment you possess, which was given you, under the guidance of prophecy, through the laying on of the hands of the elders as a body. Make these matters your business and your absorbing interest, so that your progress may be plain to all. Persevere in them, keeping close watch on yourself and your teaching; by doing so you will further the salvation of yourself and your hearers. (I Tim. 4:14–16, NEB)

There is a popular saying: "To aspire to leadership is an honourable ambition." Our leader, therefore, or bishop, must be above reproach. (I Tim. 3:1, NEB)

We beg you . . . to acknowledge those who are working so hard among you, and in the Lord's fellowship are your leaders and counsellors. Hold them in the highest possible esteem and affection for the work they do. (I Thess. 5:12–13, NEB)

Obey your leaders and defer to them; for they are tireless in their concern for you, as [those] who must render an account. Let it be a happy task for them, and not pain and grief, for that would bring you no advantage. (Heb. 13:17, NEB)

Are Bishops Necessary?

Given our self-conscious commitment to reformed rather than catholic expressions of Christianity, to the gathered-voluntary church rather than the national-parish church, why then should we bother with the concept of bishop? Why deal with a ministerial title which has been subject over the centuries to interpretations of centralized authority, and which has been supported at various periods of history by much grandeur and special privilege?[76]

One reason for dealing with bishops is purely formal. If the concept of the "gift of administration" is best understood in reference to those Biblical terms which signified congregational recognition of the gifts and offices related to the gifts, then we cannot ignore the term "bishop." Without any doubt it was one such term for ministry. While elders were appointed, probably as groups of persons in each congregation, the evidence suggests that *individual* bishops were related either to single congregations or to a group of congregations. The term "bishop" is probably the Biblical term *most* analogous to our common usage of the term "minister." It was *the* term applied to the formal leader of congregational life.

Another reason for dealing with the term "bishop" is a somewhat less formal one. If we utilize a dialectical theological method, we cannot automatically exclude terms that represent extreme, polar distortions. They may well be terms that upon examination will illumine a critical tension contained within the role of the minister-administrator.

Finally, we must consider bishops because so many Christian denominations use the designation for at least some clergy. All persons interested in ecumenical discourse ought to begin at least by being prepared to know what others see as the value of each concept related to ministry. The alternative is to begin discussion with either a closed mind or a vacant mind. Neither type of mind supports productive dialogue.

Biblical Insights on Bishops

In each of the central images of ministry through administration that we have considered in these chapters, we have referred to one of the Gospels as making a significant contribution to the understanding of that particular image. In the case of the image of bishop, we turn to the Gospel of Mark.

In many ways this is an odd place to look for help in understanding the role of bishops. It is necessary to reemphasize the way in which the Gospels are being used in this enterprise. In one sense, one could argue that the Gospels should be the last place to look in a discussion of the *office* of ministry. The Gospels were not written to assist the church in understanding its developing institutional life. Indeed, many would argue that they stand in direct opposition to it. They have little direct reference to any of the offices of the church. After all, they were only intended to cover the life, death, and resurrection of our Lord, Jesus Christ. It is in The Acts of the Apostles, the epistles, and the later New Testament writings that explicit reference is made to developing church life and the appointment of officers and leaders for the community of believers.

While we have referred regularly to insights from The Acts, the epistles, and other New Testament sources, we have made an effort also to relate the discussion to the Gospels. This is to keep the good news as revealed in Jesus as the Christ as a constant reference point. The Gospels were meant to illumine the many-faceted character of our understanding of the revelation in Christ. The church chose for the canon four attempts to describe those facets through related and yet distinct accounts of the gospel. Scholars have struggled to understand the interrelationships as well as the unique contributions of each of the writers. Our reference to the Gospels is meant to be both analogical and disciplined. As the canon supports the use of different facets to enrich our understanding of the gospel, so we are using different facets to understand the distinct and yet related functions performed by the minister of Jesus Christ.

Paradoxically, we introduce Mark in relation to the role of bishop because it is a denial of all that for which bishops have traditionally stood. We do it to state at the outset that assuming the role of bishop is to assume a permanent "position in question." However much we seek to uphold the place of order, which is represented by bishops, they *must* live with a sense of freedom or anarchy about their office. All bishops worthy of the title must have a sense of unease about their office. Of all people, bishops are tempted to think of themselves as having greater importance than they ought to think, and Mark stands as a hurdle that cannot be cleared. Mark is the "Gospel of the bishop," for it is a constant reminder to the bishop of the finitude and sin of all human life.[77] Mark enriches the meaning and implications of Acts 20:28 and I Tim. 4:16 where the Biblical writers admonish the bishop to "keep watch over yourself." However, lest we leave the tension under which a bishop lives at such a high level that it cannot be borne (and we are sure that some should not try to be bishops because the weight of the burden is beyond their tolerance), we now refer to the passages with which this chapter began.

It *is* an "honorable ambition" (I Tim. 3:1) to be a bishop. This is *not* because the position holds social esteem, approval, and endorsement. Rather, it is because the honor is a sense of regard for the person who is willing, by the grace of God, to take on the role that produces a high level of tension between the necessity of order and the demands of Christian discipleship. Everyone else in the fellowship can argue that they have a sense of freedom from the ordered "necessities" of the institutional church, whether or not they have fulfilled the demands of discipleship. Only the bishop is fully bound as a person to the institution. All persons, other than the bishop, can choose discipleship over institutional responsibility; the bishop cannot. The bishop alone must bear the tension.

The author of I Thessalonians *does* acknowledge that being a bishop is "hard work" (I Thess. 5:12). It is not hard because there are many things to do; rather, it is psychically and physically draining to live with the tension just described. As a consequence many bishops avoid the truly "hard work" of living with the tension by exhausting themselves physically in the manifold tasks which *appear* to the onlooker to be "hard work." Such work, while filling time, is actually easy work when compared with the tension described above.

The author of Hebrews has recognized the tension by pointing to the tireless character of the work and the necessity of "rendering an account." That author also asks the nonbishops to grant forms of deference in order that the bishop may know happiness rather than "pain and grief," which will help neither the bishop nor the nonbishop (Heb. 13:17). This passage might well be the "bishops' hidden text" to lighten the heart. For they could not use it openly lest they be understood as falling into the trap of self-aggrandizement by asking all nonbishops to give them obedience.

Formality and Liberty

We ask again, Are bishops necessary? If the question means, "Do all churches need to have formally recognized bishops?" the answer is clearly, "No!" The author of Mark did not intend that the church should face its crisis by appointing bishops or anything like them. Many Christian denominations down through history have sought varying ways of maintaining more-or-less radical patterns of total equality by rejecting paid clergy, by refusing to use such terminology as "bishops" for persons who exercise whatever limited form of leadership that denomination recognizes, and by developing organizational patterns that strive for balances of power and rotational patterns of leadership.

However, if the question means, "Is it necessary that some person(s) be designated in some way to exercise the function of organizing and guiding the activities of the group of Christians?" the answer is just as clearly, "Yes!" The evidence is overwhelming that no human group can function for long without addressing the issue of leadership. The church is no exception.

To bring plans and policies to fruition requires the designation of persons to organize and oversee the process. In the present discussion we call "bishops" those persons designated by the group to carry responsibility on behalf of the group for organization and oversight. In this sense, all parish ministers are bishops.

However, persons so designated can overvalue the formal elements of their positions with resulting ego problems. In developing detailed objectives and strategies, leaders can believe that their plans are beyond question. The persons who designate bishops can overvalue their decision and assign too much responsibility to the bishop, and usually also, at the same time, too many perquisites to the office. These are illustrations of placing a distorted emphasis on the "formal" side of the role of "bishops."

To counterbalance this formalism, we must recognize the place of freedom in the bishop's function. A number of theologians recognize this theological tension between freedom and order, but it is particularly seen in the way Tillich deals with the "ambiguity of legal form."[78] Every form that is adopted becomes a hindrance to the purpose the form was designed to fulfill.

Retreating into "anarchy" will not solve the problem. A bishop who develops no objectives or strategies is a whimsical tyrant, a benevolent dictator, or an ineffective leader. A bishop without objectives has no basis for communication with the members of the group being led. People allowing a bishop to function without public objectives and strategies abdicate their own responsible participation in the fulfillment of group purposes and objectives.

Within the function of bishop the greatest sense of tension, the highest possibility of prejudice, the most numerous traps, and the widest opportunity to serve are to be found. The minister as bishop is "administrator" writ large, with all of the problems, opportunities, and traps writ equally large.

Above all, bishops must work with their forms as though they were ultimate, but always function in relation to them as though they were to be abandoned at any moment. Only if bishops can affirm both formality and anarchy will they know any sense of true Christian freedom.

How then can bishops function within this tension, without either being captured by the forms and acting like dictators, or abandoning formal leadership altogether? To begin an answer to this question we turn to certain tools that have become important in modern administrative disciplines.

Tools for the Bishop's Work

When the minister as bishop begins to search for ways to make the work of the congregation productive and to help its members experience a sense of achievement, all of the prejudices against bishops reemerge, except that they reemerge with greater intensity. It was all well and good to be engaged as an elder in clarifying the main objectives of the church. That, after all, was "theological" work. The minister was trained for that. But now the congregation expects the minister as bishop to assist it in bringing those grand statements into some reality.

We will suggest that to do so involves more "administration" rather than less! We believe that accomplishment does not just happen through proper "willing" on the part of the minister. The work of the church does not happen through preaching (though constant reassertion of the agreed objectives in sermonic discourse is certainly appropriate). It cannot be "delegated" to someone else ("Oh, if we only were big enough to have a full-time church administrator, or more secretaries, or a larger staff with whom I could share all of this!"). It will not happen without attention to details and constant oversight.

The prejudices are there so soon! Being a "bishop" seems to place too much emphasis on doing and too little on believing. It involves many small things rather than the "big picture." It is not as easy as one might have thought it was going to be. It involves more training, and most of us wanted to be "doing ministry"! "Take up your tools and work" is the only response that can be made to these objections, and they are present in most of us!

A rather humble analogy can be seen in pursuing the hobby of woodworking. Woodworking is very different from what a minister normally does. It involves things rather than people, and physical rather than mental exercise. It is exciting when a new project is contemplated. The process of deciding on the project, searching many books for plans, making a final decision (usually by adapting some existing plans to one's purposes), making up the list of materials, going to the lumberyard to buy them, choosing from among all the alluring new products, bringing the materials home, getting all the tools in shape for the project, and then picking up the saw to make the first cut!

Inevitably within the first hour one of the following happens: an incorrect cut is made, ruining a whole sheet of plywood; one crucial piece of wood is missing through bad planning; or the lights go out. A normal reaction is to want to abandon the whole project! It was more complicated than it seemed. The project that was intended to help has only caused more problems!

That movement from joy to sorrow happens in the workshop, in the office, in the parish, and wherever concrete projects are attempted. The only worse situation would be to undertake a significant woodworking project without material resources or proper tools. Our goal here is briefly to describe some of the tools, some of the resources needed, and some of the experience necessary to function as a bishop. They are not the only tools possible, though we have found them to be helpful. They probably will be improved over time and even replaced, but they, or some like them, are crucial to making the work of the minister as bishop productive.

Management by Objectives

Administrative developments have moved from emphasis upon the bureaucratic and authoritative to concerns for human relations and attempts to develop more of an "open systems" theory. Persons in parish ministry have already appropriated much of this thought in a variety of ways. Leaders, in a variety of training contexts, have been prepared to work with small groups. Ministers have been encouraged to be "enablers," and the "ministry of the laity" has been stressed. All these efforts have had important results, but they also appear to be subject to their own distortions and pitfalls.

Small-group techniques can often provide an excellent context for group therapy, but they also often fall short of facilitating goals beyond the therapeutic ones. Ministers who see themselves as "enablers" frequently abandon formal leadership as such and expect that more "openness" on their part will have a magical effect upon group cohesion and goal achievement. Too many ministers also seem to believe that constant repetition of the phrase, "the ministry of the laity," as a rhetorical point, will produce a congregation of committed and functioning Christians.

No particular tool will ever fulfill all needs, and every tool can be misapplied. However, a useful administrative tool from contemporary management commends itself as a means for working within the tension of freedom and anarchy. It is "Management by Objectives" (MBO). MBO is a procedure for developing objectives and goals of performance for all members of a work group. Responsibilities are outlined and agreed upon in a participating fashion.

MBO is one means of moving from abstractions about leadership to actual leadership. Properly used, it is one effective way of organizing group activity without ignoring contributions from persons within the group. It is one way of assisting congregations in the difficult task of translating somewhat nebulous Christian goals and policies into accomplishable tasks. And it gives the minister as bishop a basis for continuing, modifying, or abandoning programs within the life of the congregation. Not *all* aspects of ministry are addressed by MBO, but the issues of organizing and overseeing the programmatic life of the congregation are.[79]

In applying MBO techniques we need to recognize the differences between congregations and the business enterprises in which the system developed. Perhaps the most crucial difference is that most persons with whom a minister works are voluntary participants while most persons with whom the business manager works are paid employees of the corporation. A second major difference is that many of the goals in business are quite easily quantifiable, and most of the goals in the life of a congregation are not. A third major difference is that a business appears to have a great many ways in which to hold persons accountable for their actions while the congregation appears to have very few such controls.

These differences will mean that an easy translation of the MBO system into congregational life will probably not be possible, but the differences are not so severe that there is no possibility of applying MBO to the congregational situation. Actually, the MBO system was developed to address some very interesting problems in business that relate to the differences just described.

In the first place, MBO grew out of the manager's concern to develop a "voluntary" motivation on the part of persons being supervised. Paid associates are not necessarily motivated associates. One major reason for using MBO in business contexts is that it stresses the participation of all parties involved, so that there is a maximum motivation on the part of all. Secondly, while a great many goals in business are quantifiable, modern managers have come to see that in the day-to-day functioning of their roles and the roles of others, it is difficult to quantify and specify the results expected from each person. Finally, combining participation and accountability is a major purpose of MBO. While not all businesses may be ready for that, most congregations probably are.

Arthur Deegan has suggested that certain conditions are essential before MBO should even be tried. If managers are not likely to trust the judgment of subordinates, the system will not work. As Deegan has written:

> The introduction of responsibility accounting, the delegation of more authority to subordinate supervisors, deliberate use of more group approaches to problem-solving and decision-making, more effective use of committee structures, widening staff meetings . . . to include more levels of supervision—these are among the techniques available and likely to be helpful in preparing the way for MBO.[80]

Given the voluntary character of congregations, the widespread emphasis on small-group dynamics, and efforts to develop the ministry of the laity, ministers probably already utilize a great many group techniques. They may already have a very wide base of decision-making. If so, the climate is appropriate for MBO, especially since the problem facing the minister as bishop is not a problem of trust, but rather of how to achieve participation *and* accountability at the same time.

The Program-Planning and Budgeting System

Another tool that has been found helpful, especially in nonprofit organizations, is the Program-Planning and Budgeting System (PPBS). Many other business management tools have assumed certain profit measurements that simply do not exist in not-for-profit organizations. Yet these not-for-profit organizations need a means of organizing and controlling activities toward other-than-profit ends.

PPBS uses a financial budget as the central focus for the process. In churches, as in educational institutions and government agencies, the budget becomes a critical point of discussion and frequent conflict. All members of a congregation recognize that there will be limited fiscal resources with which to carry out the programs of the congregation. Yet different groups within the church will argue for a change in the proportional distribution of those resources. The trustees want higher proportions spent on building maintenance, the Christian education committee sees its proportion as far too small, while the clergy relations committee was hoping to have a substantial increase for the minister's salary. What PPBS does is to relate *programs to budget,* programs being defined as "all of the functional and auxiliary services which must be undertaken to accomplish each end product or service."[81] In implementing a PPBS system, one seeks to provide "assessments of the consequences, in terms of estimated costs and benefits, or alternative program decisions."[82]

The system of PPBS, like MBO, puts a great deal of emphasis on the planning process. Specific goals are required from all responsible persons. These goals are related to particular programs to be undertaken or continued, the programs are specified in terms of financial and human resources needed, and the expected benefits are projected. While one cannot or should not designate all of the expected benefits in quantifiable terms, every effort is directed to quantifying as much as possible. The financial budget is by definition one very specific illustration of that quantification.

Objectifying both costs and benefits as they relate to particular programs provides decision makers with a basis for comparing relative benefits from different types of programs. A PPBS type of organizational framework helps to locate disagreements and conflicts around programs rather than personalities and prejudices. It facilitates intergroup communication during the decision-making process.

A common problem in church budgeting is that often the budget is constructed according to "line item" expenditures rather than according to programs undertaken. For example, the items would appear in a list such as the following: minister's salary, minister's fringe benefits, heat and light, office supplies, curriculum, building and grounds, youth program, social action projects, denominational assessments, mission giving. Such a list, while common, makes meaningful decision-making difficult. It is a strange mixture of persons, buildings, and programs. What a PPBS system does is to provide a means for allocating *all costs* to the *programs* that the church undertakes. Thereby it assists all concerned to decide if they are in fact allocating resources proportionally to the objectives that the church has decided to undertake. Where do paid staff persons spend their time in terms of programs? What programs use the buildings and to what proportion of the total cost? Which programs have additional expenses beyond paid staff and buildings? These questions are asked, answered, and become a part of the budget-making process in PPBS. The projections in the resultant budget are usually quite different from what everyone previously thought were the relative costs for particular programs. The PPBS system also allows for "feedback" during the budget year and provides for necessary adjustments as experience is compared with the earlier projections. To use the system properly involves various activities during the entire fiscal year. It provides a basis for communication between leaders at all critical points of decision-making, not just during budget construction. Alvin J. Lindgren and Norman Shawchuck have written with clarity about introducing PPBS within a congregation,[83] and we advise anyone wishing to test its value to examine their work.

One difficulty in budgeting that churches share with education, service, and government organizations is the high percentage of cost given over to paid staff and building maintenance. How is that held within bounds? How are these high cost items in fact being used? The PPBS system begins to give perspective by assigning *all* costs to particular programs. Technically this budgeting process is called "reallocation." It involves a rough calculation of staff time and building usage time by program and then reallocating that calculation to particular programs. What percentage of time does a clergyperson spend in the conduct and preparation of worship services, what percentage is spent in the work of the various committees, what percentage in calling, what percentage in denominational affairs, etc.? These percentages are simply assigned proportional costs and allocated to agreed upon programs.

In the process of reallocation, some interesting insights usually occur. Ministers are required to make some approximation of how they spend their time. This discipline involves self-evaluation and often discussion of ministers' time usage with leaders of their congregations. It is all done in relation to previously agreed upon congregational goals and objectives and therefore normally results in more realistic self-expectations by clergy and more realistic expectations of clergy by congregational leaders. The same process applied to the use of buildings and maintenance costs likewise normally reveals a much more realistic appraisal of actual costs of programs than anyone realized prior to employing a system like PPBS.

Charting

Time is a major concern for all persons with administrative responsibility. What minister has not said frequently, "Too much is being expected of me!" "There are not enough hours in the day!" "I am behind!" Such statements, which may well have elements of truth about them, quickly deteriorate into statements like, "I am going to find something where there is more control exercised over my time so that I will know when I am finished with my work and can truly relax," or, "Ministry in local congregations is impossible," or, even in moments when the pressures become internalized, "I am not any good, I can't measure up, and I might just as well give up—this church, this calling, or even this life!"

While feelings of desperation and depression need far more than simple techniques for resolution, we believe there is at least a broad need for reality testing. Time spent in evaluating what must be done, how much time is available to do it, and what can realistically be expected to be accomplished today, is not time wasted but time saved. The ministerial task *can* be interpreted as endless. Expectations of the minister by other persons *can* be unrealistic. However, ministers often resist bringing some order and realism into play. The reasons may be partially psychological, as Dittes maintains, but we assume that ministers *do* wish to "pick up their pallets and walk."

One way to bring order into the multiple expectations of ministry is to use some form of charting. At its most simple level, charting is nothing more than making a graphic presentation of the flow of work expected.[84] Some systems are simple modifications of calendars (types of Gantt Charts). Others are more sophisticated flow charts using symbols for activities as well as a time line. There are more complex models which include forms of evaluation, alternative activities dependent upon unpredictable outcomes, etc. This form of charting has been developed into a Program Evaluation and Review Technique (PERT).

Regardless of the sophistication one wishes to utilize, all forms of charting accomplish several objectives important for the work of ministers as bishops. First of all, it encourages them to allocate in advance sufficient time for tasks that are essential to the ongoing life of the congregation. It encourages them to forecast their own work and allocate appropriate time blocks. It also encourages them to break down complex tasks into elements which indicate that more time is necessary than was previously anticipated. Charting also permits them to get their agenda on the calendar. Too often, bishops allow situations to develop where calendars are filled always on the basis of requests from others. The result is that prior commitments are left to "pile up" into an impossible overload.

The use of various forms of charting enables monthly agenda to have a proper lead time built into them. It assists committees and groups in developing their own priorities and in knowing to what they have committed themselves and when it must be done. All communication is assisted by reference to the graphic portrayal of overall assignments in relation to each other. Objectifying responsibilities through graphic portrayal helps to keep confusion at a minimum and focus group effort toward the agreed goals.

Order and Anarchy

Every human organization needs leadership, but that leadership is open to abuses of power. Within the framework of the church we believe that the bishop has authority to assist the congregation to center its activities and to guide it through participatory means to realize those goals which it sets for itself.

The theological tension that faces the minister as bishop is the tension between form and anarchy, or to use the Tillichian categories, the tension in the constructive functions of the churches between form affirmation and form transcendence. To affirm any particular form without seeing the finite, limited, and sinful character of that form is to let the form become profane, that is, lacking in any spiritual content. It is, in Tillich's words, "formalistic emptiness." On the other hand, to imagine that leadership can be exercised without reference to any form (form transcendence) is to be subject to the power of "demonic repression."

The most common tendency among ministers probably is to repress forms of management. They are more at home in the areas of the transcendent (as Dittes suggested). They are all too aware of how various management forms have been used to control the behavior of others—and the clergy do not want to give the impression of seeking to "control" anyone. Our effort has been to suggest that management experts have developed various forms that assist in organizing human group action. They do not inhibit the participation of others in the process. They do recognize human tendencies toward procrastination and confusion, and they help groups and their leaders to objectify tasks so that they can be accomplished and a legitimate sense of achievement and celebration can emerge. We have suggested MBO, PPBS, and charting as ways of sustaining order rather than chaos, form rather than anarchy.

We cannot leave this discussion, however, without acknowledging the temptation all ministers face of attaching *too much* importance to the forms they use and suggest to their congregations. All forms can easily move to the point of formalistic emptiness. They can become new kinds of "activity traps." Committee job descriptions, reports of progress, evaluations of human activities in quantifiable terms, budgets related to programs, distributions of clergy time, wall charts, and scheduling boards often can and do become ends in themselves. Congregations and congregational activities, ministers and their activities, can all become overwhelmed by paperwork.

Therefore, ministers as bishops must hold a high sense of the radical critique of all organization such as that found in the Gospel of Mark. Bishops need a sense of anarchy about the very forms which they have introduced into the lives of their congregations. Agendas are developed to be set aside when the situation calls for it. Scheduling boards are not to be held before congregations as though they had some eternal value, but rather as bases for discussion and revision. Budgets are simply means of allocating priorities tentatively related to programs. They are not rigid molds into which all human need is expected to fit. In short, bishops need a sense of humor about every form they suggest or utilize.

We believe that Dittes is right in assuming that among the clergy the greater danger is in the temptations of "demonic repression." We have therefore dealt in what will appear to many ministers to be trivial practicalities. We know that we run the risk of "formalistic emptiness." We can only report that the tools mentioned have been valuable in assisting us to take up the task of administrative leadership. We know that while we have used them we have also often ignored them at crucial points of decision-making. We have tried to maintain a sense of humor about all of them. We have often found that the teacher of a new system, or the author writing about some new innovation, has seemed to take the new idea too seriously. Each new insight needs careful examination and testing. The tools can so easily become ends in themselves. Leaders should use tools only so long as they assist a human group to focus its efforts toward the goals it decides for itself. Tools can only help a profession plagued by ambiguity to become more precise and coherent and able to communicate with other people toward common ends. Tools can only assist people in celebrating their common life together. When tools become their own ends, they are a burden, and they are to be abandoned in cheerful anarchy!

All organizers of voluntary human groups find themselves vulnerable. Ministers *are* such vulnerable leaders. They work with people who have diverse expectations of the church and of the ordained ministry. For most ordained clergy there is no "tenure" of office. Frequently such leaders are surprised to find a sudden withdrawal of congregational support and affirmation. They thought that their roles were being performed appropriately and they probably were working long hours. What went wrong?

While no set of tools can ever address all that may be involved in such a situation, frequently what was lacking was a set of tools for assisting the congregation to discuss and resolve conflicting views of their objectives. There was a need for agreed means for allocating human and physical resources to the predetermined objectives. There was a lack, not of good intentions, but of some means of monitoring time and resources in relation to the estimated allocations. Each of the tools discussed in this chapter could help prevent the sudden breakdown in communication between minister and congregation, between bishop and people. They are all measures of accountability for leaders in vulnerable situations.

We have devoted this chapter to increasing predictability

within the life of congregations. We never intended to suggest that anyone could *eliminate* crisis and unpredictability. We only meant that we can eliminate *unnecessary* ambiguity and uncertainty. The life of all administrators is made up of crises and unforeseen events. Ministers as bishops are not exceptions. They learn to live with ambiguity. May they also learn to live with an appropriate sense of form.

Chapter V

The Administrator as Deacon

> And the twelve summoned the body of the disciples and said, "It is not right that we should give up preaching the word of God to serve tables. Therefore, brethren, pick out from among you seven men of good repute, full of the Spirit and of wisdom, whom we may appoint to this duty. But we will devote ourselves to prayer and to the ministry of the word." And what they said pleased the whole multitude, and they chose Stephen, . . . and . . . (Acts 6:2–5)

> Whoever would be great among you must be your servant. . . . (Matt. 20:26)

> Deacons likewise must be serious, not double-tongued, not addicted to much wine, not greedy for gain; they must hold the mystery of the faith with a clear conscience. And let them also be tested first; then if they prove themselves blameless let them serve as deacons. (I Tim. 3:8–10)

> To all the saints in Christ Jesus who are at Philippi, with the bishops and deacons. . . . (Phil. 1:1)

Most of the clergy have difficulty accepting administrative responsibilities. This observation has considerable history. It is hardly a new phenomenon of the twentieth century. In the book of Acts we read that the twelve apostles were faced with two problems: (1) the increasing number of disciples, which was causing more need for administration; and (2) conflict within the church concerning the distribution of alms to the widows. Like contemporary clergy, the apostles first reacted to such problems by suggesting that they were called to preach and *not* to become servants at table! One wonders how they could take this stand when their Master is recorded to have said, "Whoever would be great among you must be your servant, and whoever would be first among you must be your slave." In any event, their solution was to ask the congregation to select seven men of high repute to serve as deacons.

One of those so selected was named Stephen. Paradoxically, Stephen did not distinguish himself as a deacon. Instead he was a gifted preacher and a worker of signs and wonders, functions to which he did not have congregational selection or apostolic appointment. He became the first martyr, not as a result of his diaconal work, but as a result of his preaching. It must have been difficult for the disciples to realize that one appointed to the lowly function of serving tables should become the first Christian to sacrifice his life for his faith. It was one of the first *deacons* who thus gave the example of living what one preaches, *not* one of the preachers or apostles!

There is more to the story of the original appointment of deacons. They were appointed by the apostles because of internal congregational disharmony concerning distributive justice. It seems that the fellowship had been following the practice of insuring that the widows of the earliest Christians were taken care of first. After all, the Jewish Christians were the "oldest" and "founding" members of the congregation and would therefore seem to have some rights of priority. The newer expansion of the congregation involved the introduction of Greek-speaking persons into the fellowship, and their widows were being neglected in the daily distribution. Rather than first trying to determine whether or not the charges of the Hellenists were true, the apostles followed a somewhat time-honored response to group disharmony by making appointments that gave power to the newcomers. If Hellenists were put in charge of daily distribution, then presumably other Hellenists would not be likely to claim the allocation of alms to be unfair. The issue had arisen because of the expansion of the congregation through the introduction of non-Jews. Had the early church confined its membership to Jewish Christians, presumably no charges of maldistribution of the alms would have arisen. However, there would have been the issue of specialized functions among congregational leaders as the fellowship grew in size. The apostles saw preaching as a higher priority than serving.

What is fascinating in this earliest account of the appointment of deacons is the way in which service and congregational expansion are intertwined. Success in reaching the "outsider" with the content of the Christian Gospel creates internal problems of administration. In addition, an apparently wise solution to the internal problem creates still more complex problems in relating to outsiders. Deacon Stephen's preaching was alienating to synagogue members who were also conscious of problems of accommodation between Jewish beliefs and the Hellenistic culture. These Jews challenged Stephen on his interpretation of the Christian religion. Because they could not counteract his responses to their challenges, fake charges were leveled against him.

This early New Testament account raises for us several important issues that should concern us when we discuss the ministry of deacons. The first is to recognize the complexities of justice related to "serving" those within the household of believers. What are the real "needs" among members? How should the resources of the community of believers be allocated so that the needs are met with equity? Are there needs that call for attributive justice rather than distributive justice?

The second issue to recognize is that growth by the addition of new members is likely further to complicate matters of service and may well call for new forms of organization. When does the presence of persons of a different social class, race, or ethnic background call for reassessment of how the congregation has always done its business or conducted its programs?

A third issue stems from the Christian admonition to "serve" those outside the community of believers. It is difficult in principle to separate the issue of serving so-called "basic human needs" of nonmembers (hunger, sickness, imprisonment, etc.) from the desire also to share with all persons the content of the Christian message. Is there not always present a fundamental double desire on the part of the Christian to be both physical healer and spiritual evangelist at the same time? This double motivation of ministry is inherent within the Christian tradition taken as a whole.

Ministry Is Service

Before examining each of these issues in some detail, we will place the concept of the minister as deacon within the larger framework of our general thesis. We have maintained that ministry occurs *in* and through administration. This is different from saying that administration *serves* ministry or that administrative insights may be used to *manage* ministry. Until the ordained clergy recognize that administration is a central locus *of* ministry and *is* itself ministry, there will be no central motivation, either for them or for others within the community of believers, to exercise administrative functions with sensitivity and joy. We have looked at three Biblical terms that have been used to define particular forms of ministry: stewards, elders, and bishops. In each case, we have employed the term as an organizing center for functions that the community of believers has recognized as needing to be fulfilled on behalf of the community itself.

The community is a *steward* in relation to God's gifts of creation; it must find ways to *coordinate* those gifts in relation to one another. The community both acts upon, and receives from, the environment that surrounds it. The community of faith has been constituted by the revelation of God, especially in Jesus as the Christ. In the constantly changing "present," the church must examine the past traditions of the revelation for ways in which that past ought to inform the present and even more particularly the future. Which *re-formulations* of the revelation are most appropriate in living out one's stewardship? How are policies to be decided and plans for implementing them made? This *planning* function, focused in living between tradition and reformation, we have defined as the communal role of *elder.* Coordination and planning, however, are nothing if they do not result in *organized* and controlled behavior. This communal function of bringing the plans into actualization we have called the function of the *bishop.* Because we are creatures and communities in finite time and particular space, the bishop's leadership must involve the utilization of cultural forms of activity and action. But just as we acknowledge the necessity of using such forms, we also recognize the transitory and conditional character of all forms. So there should be a sense of freedom to transcend any particular forms.

In all the discussion to this point we have never fully addressed the question of the end toward which the various forms of ministry through administration are aimed. There is a sense in which coordinating, planning, and organizing are "process words." They can be, and often are, words that lack any meaningful definition of "why" the activity is entered into. They are words subject to the negative interpretation of administrative functions having no "valuation" and no purpose other than maintaining the organization itself. Therefore, stewards, elders, and bishops may well perform their assigned roles without any meaningful evaluation.

The function of the *deacon* provides the end toward which all of the other functions are aimed. The diaconal role provides the valuation for the other three. The dictionary definition of the deacon as "*(a)* clergyman below priest; *(b)* the layman dealing with secular affairs of the church,"[85] is a condescending and subordinated definition at best. The deacon is *the* minister and is concerned with the most important affairs of the church. The one who serves human need is the one who follows the calling of the Suffering Servant as incarnate in Jesus Christ.

Since our expressed goal is to explicate the *ministry* that is in *administr*ation, the word "deacon" is the *evaluative* term. Linguistically, "deacon" is the root term for "ministry." Unless a serving function is performed, there is finally no ministry at all!

The Tension Between Truth and Adaptation

A great deal of debate has been focused in recent years on the "mission" of the church. Sometimes that debate has been between "maintenance" of the institutional church and its concern for others. When the debate has centered in the maintenance-mission dichotomy, the advocates of mission normally have stressed the socially transforming role of the church. They have argued for more emphasis on secular political processes, efforts to make the social system more "liberating" or more "responsible," or on efforts to develop church programs aimed at the rights of the socially dispossessed. At other times people have debated the definition of the word "mission" itself. In this case the argument has been focused on what is to be done for those outside the membership of the church. Some, normally referring to themselves as "evangelicals," have argued by word and deed that the mission of the church is evangelism, that is, seeking to assist the non-Christian (or lapsed Christian) to have a conversion experience and thus know the reality of God's justification of the sinner through the ministry and mediation of Jesus Christ and the Holy Spirit.

The less evangelistic Christians have given priority to sanctificationist rather than justificationist themes. They argue that Christians, having known God's justification, ought *then* to act in a caring manner for the needs of all of God's children whether converted or not. These Christians most often seek change in social systems rather than seeking change in individual religious perceptions or meeting the needs of particular individuals. Recently even the nonevangelistic denominations have been trying to develop programs of evangelism (by which is meant the search for new members).

We have no illusions that this debate can be easily resolved, nor do we wish to argue that the debate is not an important one between denominations, within denominations, and even within congregations. We do wish to suggest, however, that on whichever side of the debate one finds oneself, there is a common paradox faced by the advocates of each position. The apostles faced it when they appointed Stephen and the other deacons, and Stephen faced it as he sought to address himself in the name of Christianity to the other Hellenists.

Paul Tillich associates this paradox with the expansion functions of the churches: "the polarity of the principles of verity and adaptation."[86] In order to expand, the church—which exists by virtue of a truth claim which it has received (verity)—must in some way adapt itself and that truth to the new people and new situations it wishes to influence. If it, mistakenly, holds that the truth as the church has traditionally proclaimed it needs no adaptation to reach the new persons, the church is subject to "a demonic absolutism which throws the truth like stones at the heads of people, not caring whether they can accept it or not."[87] "If, on the other hand, the adaptation becomes unlimited accommodation . . . , the message's verity is lost, and a relativism takes hold of the church which leads to secularism, first merely empty and without ecstasy, but later open to demonically distorted ecstasy."[88]

In the story of Stephen we see both verity and adaptation at work. The church wisely sought an adaptive structure through which to deal with the situation of Hellenistic widows, a situation that had resulted from the church's expansion. Stephen sought in his sermon to affirm the truth claims of Christianity as he saw them through his Hellenistic eyes. In this case, it appears that the adaptation had not been empty, and the truth as proclaimed was not demonically absolute.

Service *is* the form of expansion and mission for the

church. If there is any mission at all, be it to individuals or to social structures, be it in the form of spiritual evangelization or of meeting physical human needs, the church must adapt its own structure of maintenance and the message proclaimed. Assuming that the message and structure are interrelated, the tension of truth and adaptation is *the* diaconal tension.

We turn then to an examination of this diaconal tension in the three issues identified above in the story of Stephen.

What Is Just Distribution?

Our first concern is to discuss the "service" to those in need within the community of believers, for that was the need which the original deacons were appointed to serve. At first glance, that seems like a simple enough task. Who would turn away from fellow believers who were in obvious physical need? As any practicing minister will readily confess, however, the problem is not simple at all. What proportion of the church's total material resources should be set aside to help those who have material needs? What does one do when many—if not most—people in contemporary congregations will be offended rather than joyful at being designated recipients of material charity?

If one moves beyond obvious material needs, the problems become even more complex. How much time should the leaders of the congregation give to persons in need of counseling? What proportion of the time available for visitation should they devote to the sick, to the elderly, to the lonely, or to "regular" pastoral visitation, which often reveals needs previously unknown? Every congregation has its share of "problem" persons who will absorb (or "demand") seemingly endless hours of ministerial time. When should the minister as deacon say, "Enough time has been given to this man, for his needs are beyond meeting"? And none of these questions have even addressed the changed congregational structure and programs due to the addition of new "types" of people as a result of congregational expansion.

Final answers to such questions can never be given, but we can point to directions for seeking tentative resolutions. The first such direction is to distinguish between distributive and attributive justice in meeting human need. Since every human being in some way needs the ministry of the church, attention must be given to the allocation of time, energy, and human resources to seeking out and meeting those needs. Whatever the technique or tool employed (be it "general" pastoral and diaconal calling, cottage meetings distributed throughout the congregation, systematic retreats, or programmed "listening sessions" with congregational leaders), time and energy must be allocated on an equal justice principle based on the fundamental equality of human need. The techniques must be genuine efforts to ask each member of the church, "What can we do to meet your particular form of need?" Without recognizing the universality of human need, the minister as deacon is likely to assume that the congregation can be divided into those capable of "serving" and those "needing to be served." Each of us, rather than being in one group or the other, remains a "commuter" between the two groups, both serving and being served.

Exclusive appeal to the principle of distributive justice, however, would not only be foolish; it would also be unchristian. Every congregational leader knows that, at any particular moment in time, some members of the household of believers are taking inordinate and disproportionate amounts of time and energy in "being served." To continue serving them is to appeal to the principle of attributive justice: giving more on the basis of greater need. However, what are the limits to such an attributive appeal? Are there any? Some schools of psychiatry would say there are no limits. A psychiatrist simply builds up a clientele that fills the available time, and goes on serving those people as long as they are capable of bearing the cost. The pattern is not quite the same for clergy, for the persons using the time of the clergy do not normally bear the cost. But many clergy do exert a major portion of their energy serving cases of dramatic need for many, many months at a time. It seems appropriate, with the advice and consent of fellow deacons within the congregation, to set tentative limits to the exercise of attributive forms of diaconal service. When the tentative limits are being reached (such as six counseling sessions, or the allocation of a particular dollar amount of material aid, or weekly visitation for a month), the situation is then sensitively reviewed with the participation of the person "being served." Have we reached a meaningful place to change the pattern? Are there other forms of service available? Is any progress being made? Who needs to help with this decision? To which other "deacons" should we turn?

One could well argue that if such patterns are not established, the minister as deacon is in danger of encouraging "spiritual hypochondria." With such difficult decisions as the termination of service, it is well to seek counsel from fellow deacons. Adequate protections for confidentiality can be established in such consultative situations.

Sharing internal congregational concerns for distributive and attributive expressions of diaconal service with a "board of deacons" can be, and often is, an example of exciting and creative administration. Far too often the "deacons" confine themselves to decisions concerning the frequency of "serving tables" at Holy Communion and the proper distribution of the special Christmas offering. Such matters clearly are appropriate agenda items for such a group, but they hardly express a creative "vision of diaconal service."

In meeting internal needs for service to the membership, the diaconal tension then presents itself as the "veritable" principle of distributive equality over against the "adapted" principle of attributive service based on inordinate need.

Changing Structures

A second way in which diaconal service presents tension is in the need to evaluate the structures through which service is given. In the first concern we called for regular diaconal review of how resources are being devoted to cases of special need within the congregation. In the illustrations we gave, the minister as deacon used other deacons as a reference group, but no structural changes were suggested for congregational programming. In the Stephen story in Acts the early congregation did in fact introduce structural change by making it a condition of diaconal appointment that one needed to be a Hellenist. The truth remained that widows needed to be given alms.

Now this concern seems to be straightforward enough so that little or no commentary is necessary. Needed changes, however, rarely present themselves in such a simplified manner. It seems doubtful that even the early church resolved the change with the dispatch which the brief Lukan sentences in Acts seem to suggest. Such changes are usually but visible signs of much deeper stresses within the congregation. For example, the diaconal appointment described in Acts was but the visible sign of a most crucial decision: Was the Christian faith *intended* for all people, or was it to remain a Jewish sect? One almost can hear some Christian members of the time expressing some hesitancy about giving Hellenist widows their full share of alms, for, "If we do make a special effort on their behalf, we will only attract more and more Hellenists until we will have trouble finding anyone in the congregation who even knows about Moses!"

In a contemporary congregation, the same tension is likely to emerge when it is discovered how much time and effort is being devoted to serving couples with marital problems. Some deacon may well suggest that since the congregation currently has only a "couples club," there is need to organize a "single parents group," or perhaps better yet a club for the "recently divorced" or "those contemplating divorce" (or both in the same club). It would be a rare congregation in which such a suggestion would not be greeted with comments such as: "We can't do that, for this church has always affirmed the sanctity of marriage. Soon I fear this church will be nothing but divorced people." "Already we are known in this town as the church that encourages divorce!" "I know Mary and John went through a lot of pain when they were divorced, but honestly, I think Paul and Sue should have faced up to their problems rather than taking the easy way out. Besides, I heard that John and Sue are now dating and the first thing you know they will want to marry in this church."

To make the concern between truth and adaptation even more pronounced, what about the presence of avowed homosexuals in the congregation? A suggestion has been made that a homosexual coffeehouse be sponsored by the congregation since a major problem among homosexuals is that they cannot meet except in exploitive bars and nightclubs. When does the valid "truth" of covenant marriage and/or heterosexuality become demonic, and when has the "adaptation" of divorce and/or homosexuality become profane?

When does one simply "serve" need, and when does one begin to reexamine values as a result of addressing need? As long as needs are met by diaconal service that is confined to individual "caring," the real diaconal tension can be avoided. However, as soon as congregational *structure* is modified to meet such needs through *congregational* "caring," then questions of truth and adaptation *must* be addressed. One is no doubt performing "ministry" when counseling with an individual contemplating divorce or when meeting with a closet homosexual in the confines of the ministerial study. But we are suggesting that the administrative decisions regarding congregational restructuring to meet such needs *is* an even more central locus of ministry. There the diaconal tensions become more obvious, more open—and thus more painful and also more full of opportunity to deal with the full implications of ministry.

The resolution of these tensions will never finally be completed. The main point is not to suggest which way congregations should decide on matters of such tension, but rather that the existence of such structural consideration is an evaluation of effective ministry. If a congregation is not evaluating its ministry through debates concerning the appropriateness or inappropriateness of structural modifications that have emerged from diaconal ministries, it is probably not having an effective ministry.

Double Serving

The third concern that emerged from the Stephen story was the Christian's "double desire" to meet both the physical and the spiritual needs of the non-Christians (or the lapsed Christians) who are outside the community of believers. Here the verity/adaptation tension presents itself in a somewhat different way.

Any congregation seeking to "expand its ministry" beyond those persons already within its influence does not really have the luxury of trying first to decide whether to give priority to "evangelism" or to "meeting human need." If one begins by stressing the hunger for spiritual truth that exists outside the congregation, one soon finds that new members have all too human forms of special needs. Or, if one begins by making a sociological analysis of changing community constituencies, one soon finds that the "new people" reached want to know how the church will address their "religious" needs and not just who they are as sociological creatures. Needless to say, not all persons reached through "evangelism" will immediately present to the congregation their physical and human needs, nor will all of those who originally are reached through the addressing of human needs immediately ask for "spiritual" enrichment. Whichever form of "outreach" a congregation chooses for its emphasis, there will be reason soon enough to give attention to the wholeness of the human person and the multiplicity of form in which human need is presented.

One can see the complexity of the verity/adaptation tension in relation to this "double serving" of those presently outside the community of believers when one considers the normal reaction of the present membership to suggestions for new ways of serving those outside. Looking first at "evangelistic" efforts, we use as an example the moderately liberal, middle-class congregation. Such a congregation usually lets the clergy define the religious content of the Christian faith; the members are not accustomed to sharing their faith visions with others. In fact, they are frequently somewhat embarrassed to do so. If then such a congregation decides to reach "outsiders" through evangelistic sharing of their definitions of the Christian faith, they must first define what is the "truth" of that faith. In the process of doing so, if the use of a predetermined "formula" is rejected as a strategy, a wide range of personal "truth" statements will emerge from the members. Some will be humanistic in content, while others will tend to be conservative and fundamentalistic, with many ambiguous and even inarticulate statements ranging between these extremes.

Recently, at a meeting of the board of deacons of a large metropolitan liberal congregation just such an exercise was undertaken. All of the deacons wrote brief sentences describing their basic faith reasons for being members of that congregation. When the anonymous responses were read aloud there was a mixed reaction of astonishment, joy, and depression. The range of variation was beyond anyone's expectation. The group felt exhilarated to know of the beliefs present within the group, but they were also depressed with what could be done with such a range of statements. There were frequent comments of, "I wish I had said it that well, for I believe that too, but did not think of it!"

A first attempt to come to some sort of a common statement resulted in little except a general agreement that everyone present believed in "love." However, as soon as certain definitions of love were suggested the group split into various "camps" supporting one definition or another. The process of seeking agreement was abandoned and it was suggested that the "truth" the congregation had to share with outsiders was that people of various beliefs could productively exist within the same congregation. This seemed to most persons present to be an excellent basis for an evangelism effort until one deacon suggested that she was uncomfortable taking such a message to anyone outside the congregation as a basis for winning new "believers." She felt that in effect she would be saying to new prospects that they should join the church *because* it didn't matter what they believed. She found it hard to see why anyone would find that a very compelling reason to join a church. She felt that most people would simply be courteous to her but inside would be thinking, "Well, why go there, since I have held my beliefs for some time without the need of a congregation? If they will just say I can believe what I want to believe, why bother to join?"

This comment elicited the statement from others that she had misinterpreted what was being said. Two people suggested that diversity produced strength and spiritual growth because the interchange of different belief statements helped one to modify and understand better what one *really* believed! These respondents used the illustration of what had just happened in the group: hearing statements from others had brought forth new insight for most persons present. The objecting deacon wisely countered with the following statement: "That's some illustration. I have been a member of this church for fifteen years and tonight is the first time I have ever been asked to state my faith or to hear someone else do it. I would feel like a liar to go out and tell new prospects that such a process is what happens in this church!" The result of the evening's discussion was the decision to announce to the congregation a series of evening "faith discussions" for members and that the deacons would invite the "new prospects" to attend these discussions. We should add that the series was quite popular in the congregation but that few new members resulted from the effort.

What has happened in this illustration? The search for a "truth" to share revealed a diverse meaning of truth latent within the congregation. Christian truths had been (appropriately or inappropriately, depending on your theological position) "adapted" over time to the American middle-class values of tolerance for diversity, independence, and freedom of expression. At least in this case, the wider effort at sharing this "adapted verity" did not reach many new prospects for the congregation. It may well have had salutary effects within the congregation by assisting it to develop programs reflective of latent needs within the membership. In all probability, the program failed to reach new persons because it reflected more the adaptation of the truth concepts to the needs of the present membership and did not sufficiently reflect appropriate adaptation to the needs of the potential membership.

Determining those spiritual needs could itself have been a possible program for the deacons. Assuming that those needs would have proven to be somewhat different from the needs of the present membership, the deacons would have had to make a decision: how far could such adaptation go before the "truths" held by present members would have been jeopardized beyond their willingness to modify them? Engaging in such an exercise would, interestingly enough, have been an example of the value of dialogue between Christian "truths," which the board of deacons had espoused as a chief attraction of the congregation.

We could build a similar scenario around congregational efforts to reach the nonchurched on the basis of more tangible rather than more "spiritual" goals. The tension between verity and adaptation remains the same. For example, the vast majority of American congregations have programs that are most attractive to persons identified with the nuclear heterosexual family of working husband, homemaking wife, and school-age children. The types of groups sponsored, the times of group meetings, the patterns of worship services, and the educational programs all reflect this particular form of adaptation. The pattern of adaptation reflects values and truths held strongly by majorities of congregational memberships. These values are sometimes consciously related to explicit Christian themes, but more often there is only an unconscious and unarticulated relationship felt within the congregation between these cultural patterns and Christian affirmations. Should the congregation be interested in "serving" divorced persons, single-parent families, career women, members of racial and ethnic groups, or avowed homosexuals, the issues of conflict between the assumed truths and proposed adaptations become acute. Indeed, it is frequently the case that congregations do not initiate such discussions and propose such programs. Instead they remain in a more reactive position; they do not act until requests come from members of one or the other of these nontraditional groups to sponsor programs aimed at serving and attracting persons from these self-conscious groupings.

The issues at stake between truth and adaptation in relation to any one of these groups are complex. It is sufficient for our purpose here simply to identify the reality of ministry found in diaconal administration which seeks to deal with these tensions. As in many of the issues of ministry in administration that we have discussed, clergy are understandably frustrated and often repelled by the depth of feelings generated within congregations by these issues. It is much less threatening to have the issues presented within the confines of personal counseling rather than in policy meetings of the board of deacons. A person in the pain of contemplated divorce or the "closet" homosexual seeking guidance from the clergy can be dealt with in a much more controlled situation than is usually the case when we discuss the diaconal responsibility to serve and attract such groups. It is also frequently the case that a counselee wishes to reflect the dominant values, when in fact the difficulty of living with those values has produced the counselee's request for help. When one seeks to serve groups of such persons, frequently the group does *not* wish to reflect the traditional values but rather hopes to achieve equal standing and recognition of the truths contained in their socially defined deviant behavior.

We believe full ministry is to be found precisely in moving into the center of these debates and tensions. There is value *both* in the assumed verity and in the requested adaptation.

As in the case of the first deacon, attracting Hellenists resulted in transformation of both the Hellenists and the traditional Jewish Christians. From the tension came a more profound understanding of what was Christian truth within Jewish Christianity and what was merely Jewish. Among the Hellenists there was a deeper appreciation of what change was necessary in becoming Christian.

Far too often clergy are tempted to solve the tension simply by affirming the need of adapting to the nontraditional group's needs or affirming the traditional values already supported by the congregation. In the first instance clergy assume the correctness of a "prophetic" position, and in the second instance they assume the correctness of extant definitions of "Christian" behavior. What is called for is the raising of questions concerning what Christianity has to bring to the newly conscious group or what the new group has to bring to the worshiping congregation. Both groups ought to be changed in the process of diaconal service. If they are not, the process has resulted in affirming one or the other pole of the verity/adaptation dialectic rather than affirming the truth of the dialectic itself.

Servant Leadership

It seems almost pathetic to put forth a problem as complex as the dialectical tension of verity and adaptation and then suggest that the main guideline for the minister as deacon in such a situation is to provide questions that emphasize the dialectic rather than provide answers. Clergy usually feel "shortchanged" by such suggestions. When dramatic cases of tension emerge within a congregation, the members expect leadership! They expect answers from the minister! Has the minister not been trained in such things? Is the minister not a professional? Contrary to popular expectation, leadership in such situations comes not from an "answer giver" but rather from one who escalates the profundity and richness of the tension that exists. A minister should not permit the group to decide too easily either for an assertion of the demonic absolutism of old truths or for the unreflective acceptance of any new group's particular interpretation of Christianity. But providing new questions for the congregation is not easily accepted as a leadership role.

Of the Synoptic Gospel writers, only Luke placed the saying of Jesus that the disciple should imitate his Lord, *the* servant, in the context of the Last Supper (Luke 22:25–27). Luke emphasized the critical import of this particular saying and placed it at the moment when the disciples ought most to have been able to hear the content. Jesus was teaching that leadership is not what it so often appears to be. It may well be the servant who "leads" the group rather than the one officially designated as leader.

By placing this saying of Jesus in the context of the Last Supper, Luke has emphasized a truth that most of us find it very difficult to accept. Yet Jesus does provide the model for such a servant leadership. How many times in the Gospel accounts is Jesus presented with a seemingly insolvable dilemma in which previous definitions of truth clash with contemporary human need? A common pattern for Jesus was not to answer the question but to present a new and deeper question either directly or through the use of a parable. It was Jesus' questions and not his answers which provided the leadership needed at such difficult moments.

Luke's Gospel also provides other norms for the minister as deacon. Luke portrays Jesus as a servant who is also a king, who redefines the very meaning of being a captive or being oppressed in terms of "suffering from disruptive forces in life."[89] Luke's Gospel is directed primarily toward the outside world,[90] and it emphasizes Jesus' love and concern for the dispossessed as well as the person accepted by society.

This universal character of Jesus' serving mission is present in episode after episode in the Lukan account. Jesus is servant and rescuer of the outcast. Jesus is serving a divine plan, which for him is the only important authority. From the Lukan account we find a diaconal ministry serving an ever-expanding circle of persons who are in need of help. For Luke the church is not a subversive sect choosing as its target the worldly powers. It is rather a universal fellowship dedicated to finding human need in all its forms and declaring through word and act the deliverance wrought in Jesus as the Christ.

Chapter VI

Admonitions to Administrators

> Having gifts that differ according to the grace given to us, let us use them. (Rom. 12:6)
>
> As each has received a gift, employ it for one another, as good stewards of God's varied grace . . . in order that in everything God may be glorified through Jesus Christ. (I Peter 4:10–11)
>
> Hence I remind you to rekindle the gift of God that is within you through the laying on of my hands; for God did not give us a spirit of timidity but a spirit of power and love and self-control. Do not be ashamed then. . . . (II Tim. 1:6–8)

The "gift of administration" or the "minister-administrator" as a unifying symbol for understanding ordained ministry will probably not gain any more popular following than H. Richard Niebuhr's "pastoral director."[91] From our point of view that is good. We have not argued for any simple conception easily captured in one term, nor have we sought to coin a new word. Ministry is far too complex in motivation, tasks, and settings for simple description. This complexity, as we have seen, has contributed both to frustration and depression and to a certain richness and depth of experience among ordained ministers. In many ways ministry is still (and perhaps now even more) the "perplexed profession" of which Niebuhr wrote in 1956.

In almost every survey of clergy this mix of frustration and satisfaction is evident. If there is a "tilt" in one direction or another, usually frustration is more pronounced than satisfaction. That was true of the newspaper interview that produced the "junk for Jesus" remark we quoted at the beginning of Chapter I. This frustration causes many clergy to be suspicious of new techniques and methods proposed to "solve" the dilemmas that clergy face. They are suspicious because they have tried out many a new idea only to discover its shallowness and limited utility in a complex professional role. This is particularly true of recommended administrative tools. We would be surprised if clergy were not suspicious of our suggestions here. Too often discussions of ministry and administration are either laden with management jargon or lacking in understanding of the complexity of ministry.

We have presented no panacea. Ministry will not be made "easy" because of anything which appears in these pages. But through the conception of the diverse functional expectations of clergy performance around the image of minister-administrator, the role of the clergy can be clarified, the dissonance between what they really do and what they ideally ought to do can be reduced, and the effectiveness of the church can be strengthened. Ministry through administration is not the latest technique to deal with the minister's "chores." It is a means for understanding the clergy role *in* the community of believers and enhancing the ministry *of* the community of believers.

In this concluding chapter we will focus on some of the issues and concerns that such ministry may raise in the minds of clergy and congregations. Our responses may be understood as cautions, warnings, or admonitions.

Include the Prophetic

Of the ministerial "offices" discussed no mention has been made of the prophetic office. This has been intentional. We have included in our Biblical analysis two specific referents: (1) the explicit references in The Acts of the Apostles, the epistles, and the later New Testament writings to developing church life and the appointment of officers and leaders for the community of believers, and (2) the Gospels, as a vehicle for addressing the many-faceted character of our understanding of the gift of administration in direct relationship to the good news revealed in Jesus Christ. This choice of Biblical referents was not made out of any disregard for Old Testament sources. Indeed, Old Testament themes such as creation, covenant, and stewardship would be rich sources for this discussion and would provide a helpful grounding for the concerns expressed in our thesis. However, we have not claimed to be making a definitive analysis but rather an illustrative interpretation of major insights. Among the many possible sources for this discussion, our focus Biblically has been on these two as being the most helpful in understanding a Biblical base for the administrative role of the minister of Jesus Christ.

Yet some may wish to argue that we have ignored the prophetic office. Is not the task of administration bound to be unrelated to that of prophetic activity? Does not a focus on the ministerial office in relationship to administration exclude the ecstatic and visionary and socially critical dimensions of ministry? We would answer, "No!" To argue that the administrative ministry excludes the prophetic is to misunderstand both.

Surely the prophets functioned with a great deal of independence from the operation of the official cult. In fact they often engaged in bitter attacks on the cult They were also integrally related to the whole body of the people, more so in certain periods than in others. Increasingly the "writing prophets," especially Amos, Isaiah, Micah, and Jeremiah, were more radical in declaring their independence from the religious establishment. However, this independence was never total. In fact, they performed an intercessory function that caused them to be seen as authorized spokespersons of the people.[92]

A contemporary illustration of the importance of this relationship between the prophet and the community with its structure and tradition is Dr. Martin Luther King, Jr. and the Southern Christian Leadership Conference. Behind his own prophetic activity was an extremely effective institution that used sophisticated administrative tools. The "I Have a Dream" speech was the consequence of an elaborately orchestrated act of ministry through administration. The impact of the civil rights movement as a whole depended upon a realistic and effective administration of strategy.

The belief that the administrative excludes the prophetic office fails to understand the concept as we have developed it. The gift of administration is not only a *centripetal* gift, drawing the minister into the very center of the community of believers—it is also a *centrifugal* gift, focusing *out from* the community and generating ministry on behalf of the world beyond the community itself. It is this centrifugal character of the gift which provides the prophetic role counteracting the tendency of any community for self-concern and self-interest.[93]

It is our belief that ministers who argue passionately for a prophetic ministry do so out of a desire to function in isolation from the community of believers. We give lip service to the "priesthood of all believers" and to the "theology of the laity," but in fact we ministers find it extremely difficult to function as elders among elders and actually prefer to work alone. The lure to power and authority and a certain independence from the community attracts us to the prophetic model. Yet we must remember that the Old Testament prophets, even those who were ecstatic and visionary and socially critical, prophesied within the context of the community of believers.

Remember the Struggling Church

It might also be argued that ministry through administration works well only in the white, middle-class, urban church. What about the small church, the rural church, the poor church? What can the "gift of administration" possibly mean in these settings, especially where all energies are directed to the struggle for survival? How can techniques of administering be at all helpful in places where the task is to "get by," "follow the Spirit," or simply "apply the gospel"?

Our objective has not been to add "techniques" to ministry but to suggest a model of ministry in and through administration. The "gift of administration" is not limited to large, urban, wealthy churches. It is just as relevant, and actually more relevant, to small, rural, poor churches and their leadership. These groups, are in fact, more likely to benefit from the concept. This may be illustrated in several ways.

In the Twin Cities of Minneapolis and Saint Paul, the Metropolitan Church Commission, through a major grant from the George D. Dayton Foundation, established for the churches in the area a project entitled "Viable Futures." The stated purpose of this project was to increase the effectiveness of the church by training local church ministers and lay leaders in planning. This involved not the simple transplanting of management techniques into local churches but the integration of planning into the mission and purpose of congregational life. One of the discoveries of this project was that the congregations which most benefited were the struggling ones. Instead of just reacting to crises, these churches discovered that with careful planning they were able to anticipate problems and deal with them in ways that were less likely to threaten the church's very survival. One further benefit was the way in which clergy and laity were helped in planning together. This increased substantially the mutuality of ministry (shared leadership of elders) and helpfully mobilized the maximum resources of the whole community of believers in facing their special needs and concerns.[94]

Another illustration comes from the minister as bishop. In struggling congregations it is often the single paid leader who bears the brunt of the responsibility (and blame) for the situation in which the church finds itself. "Oh, if only we could get an enthusiastic young minister to come in here and start attracting new members and developing some exciting programs," more than one search committee of small congregations has wished. Therefore, the ordained minister finds a readiness to move in new ways, to try new ideas, to set objectives and evaluate their accomplishments. Tools from the management disciplines may well be effective vehicles for organizing the efforts of church members and for helping them translate their wishful thinking into accomplishable tasks.

It is also the single (functioning alone) clergyperson in a single-paid-staff church who feels the peoplework/paperwork frustration the keenest. One such minister designed a whimsical curriculum for a theological seminary. The first semester included "Introduction to Typing," "Stenciling I," and "Mimeographing I"; and studies progressed from there to more advanced work in "The Minister as Errand Boy," "Principles of Church Decoration," and "Fundamentals in Church Property." This "curriculum" included "electives" in "New Testament," "Church History," "Systematic Theology," and "Homiletics," among others, but it also indicated that "the faculty has the right to limit electives, where completion of the required courses is hindered by work in religious studies."[95] While the proposal is obviously tongue-in-cheek, the frustrations of this minister with the administrative demands of operating a small church are abundantly in evidence. We believe that this sense of ministerial dissonance between what the ministry ought to be and what the actual tasks of ministry are may be reduced by using the unifying symbol of the gift of administration. This perspective, bringing together as it does the multiple expectations and tasks of the ordained clergy (perhaps most poignantly in the struggling church), can enable clergy better to understand what they are called to do and to do it with a greater sense of personal integration and confidence.

The Holy Spirit May Act in Your Administration

Not long ago one of us participated in a planning meeting for a spiritual growth retreat. It was an ecumenical venture The purpose of the meeting was to examine all dimensions of the retreat and determine what needed to be done to assure its success. The committee quickly realized the amount of work this would require. There were five denominational groups, each with its own particular concerns and agenda for the retreat. A considerable quantity of physical materials needed to be assembled. Providing food and sleeping quarters for the participants was neither simple nor inexpensive. The retreat was to be held over two weekends in a church building. This demanded careful planning so that the church's program would not be inconvenienced unduly and the building would be left in a clean and orderly condition once the retreat was over.

In the midst of the discussion several participants became quite frustrated. One of them said: "I think we should leave the weekend in God's care and try not to manage and control the Holy Spirit with all our planning. If God wants this retreat to succeed, he will make it. We're getting too concerned in this meeting with our own agenda. What about God's agenda?" This person stated a concern that often surfaces where conscious coordinating, planning, and organizing takes place in a church context. It is a concern which has as a fundamental assumption that human management and administration thwarts God's intentions and excludes the activity of the Holy Spirit.

Surely we would agree that the purposes and activity of God often are experienced in human life as the spontaneous "breaking through" that upsets and transforms a situation in profound ways. We would argue, however, that God's intentions and involvement are just as clearly evident in the midst of human administration. Operating predominantly out of a "conversionist" view of the relationship between Christ and culture, we have underscored an essentially positive view of creation and of the contributions of human culture. God's intentions for human life are embedded (albeit in a sinful and distorted fashion) in the very fabric of human culture. Far from standing back and "allowing" God to act, the human is responsible for using God-given tools to further God's purposes. "Having gifts that differ according to the grace given to us, let us use them . . ." (Rom. 12:6). God's intentions can be served by human efforts to respond faithfully to God's creative activity in our midst. Administration can be one expression of the faithful response to God.

Use Whatever Glorifies God

One frequently expressed concern about the use of administrative tools in the church is the fear of the "seductiveness" of management technique. One can become so enamored with techniques, so the argument goes, that it would be better not to risk introducing them in the first place. Could not the tools become the ends as well as the means of ministry in the church?

Clearly this *is* a risk. We are well aware of the difficulty of integrating disciplines.[96] We also know of the abuses that are possible as ministers begin to function with specific management tools. But we believe the greater danger is the rejection of forms of management because clergy are either uncomfortable with them or fearful that members of the congregation will think they are seeking to manipulate and control. While recognizing the legitimate concern about the seductiveness of management technique, we suggest two things to remember about the relationship of ministry and administration.

First, the key to the means-end problem is proportionality. The question is not, "Does the end justify any means?" It is rather, "Does this end justify these means?" or, more specifically, "Is the use of these techniques an end in itself?" or, "Do these techniques help clarify the clergy role and strengthen the effectiveness of the church?" Ministers as bishops (i.e., in the Biblical leadership role in whose functioning the administrative tools are most frequently in evidence) must always function with a sense of unease about their office and with a sense of humor about the tools they use in the execution of their tasks.[97]

Secondly, it is not a "blending" of ministry and administration which we propose. Rather, the correct relationship is a transformative one. As H. Richard Niebuhr observed of this "solution" to the problem of the relationship between Christ and culture:

> There is no phase of human culture over which Christ does not rule, and no human work which is not subject to his transforming power over self-will—as there is none, however holy, which is not subject to deformation.[98]

The contributions of human culture, in this case the tools of management, must always stand subject to Christ's rule. At issue is not the progress of human institutions through the latest technique but the conversion of the human spirit from self-serving technique to the service of God. Being sensitive, then, both to the abuses and to the redeeming possibilities of the tools of human culture, let us "employ [them] for one another, as good stewards of God's varied grace . . . in order that in everything God may be glorified through Jesus Christ" (I Peter 4:10–11).

Notes

1. H. Richard Niebuhr, *The Purpose of the Church and Its Ministry* (Harper & Brothers, 1956).

2. Ibid., p. 48.

3. H. Richard Niebuhr, *Christ and Culture* (Harper & Brothers, 1951).

4. *The Interpreter's Dictionary of the Bible* (Abingdon Press, 1962), Vol. III, p. 388.

5. Ibid.

6. Cyril Eastwood, *The Priesthood of All Believers* (London: Epworth Press, 1960), pp. ix–xii.

7. Gerhard Kittel and Gerhard Friedrich (eds.), *Theological Dictionary of the New Testament,* tr. by Geoffrey W. Bromiley, Vol. III (Wm. B. Eerdmans Publishing Co., 1965), p. 250.

8. *Interpreter's Dictionary of the Bible,* Vol. IV, p. 436.

9. T. W. Manson, *The Church's Ministry* (London: Hodder & Stoughton, 1948), p. 59.

10. Eastwood, *The Priesthood of All Believers,* pp. 66f.

11. Anthony T. Hanson, *The Pioneer Ministry* (Westminster Press, 1961), p. 124.

12. John T. McNeill, *The History and Character of Calvinism* (Oxford University Press, 1954), p. 218. Also Emanuel Stickelberger, *Calvin: A Life,* tr. by D. G. Gelzer (John Knox Press, 1954), p. 91.

13. Hanson, *The Pioneer Ministry,* p. 120.

14. Wilhelm Pauck, "The Ministry in the Time of the Continental Reformation," in H. R. Niebuhr and D. D. Williams (eds.), *The Ministry in Historical Perspectives* (Harper & Brothers, 1956), p 116.

15. Niebuhr, *The Purpose of the Church and Its Ministry.*

16. See Robert W. Lynn (ed.), "The Auburn Study of Reform in Theological Education" (1979; unpublished).

17. *From Max Weber: Essays in Sociology,* tr., ed., and with an introduction by H. H. Gerth and C. Wright Mills (Oxford University Press, 1946), p. 115.

18. Ibid., p. 134.

19. Ibid., p. 138.

20. Ibid., p. 137.

21. For an outline of the four aspects of "call," see Niebuhr, *The Purpose of the Church and Its Ministry,* pp. 84f.

22. *Readiness for Ministry,* 2 vols. (Vandalia, Ohio: American Association of Theological Schools, 1975–1976).

23. James Dittes, *Minister on the Spot* (Pilgrim Press, 1970).

24. Paul Tillich, *Systematic Theology,* 3 vols. (University of Chicago Press, 1951–1963).

25. Tillich, *Systematic Theology,* Vol. III, p. 82.

26. Niebuhr, *The Purpose of the Church and Its Ministry,* pp. 79f.

27. Ibid., p. 81.

28. Kittel, *Theological Dictionary of the New Testament,* Vol. III, p. 1036.

29. Hanson, *The Pioneer Ministry,* p. 62.

30. Daniel Jenkins, *The Gift of Ministry* (London: Faber & Faber, 1947), pp. 59–62.

31. A strong example of such a book would be Alvin J. Lindgren and Norman Shawchuck, *Management for Your Church* (Abingdon Press, 1977).

32. Peter Rudge, *Ministry and Management* (London: Tavistock Publications, 1968).

33. Rudge's serious attempt at correlation of theology of ministry and management has been used by other authors (Lindgren and Shawchuck) and has proved to be helpful. However, certain flaws emerge when we examine Rudge carefully. By the very nature of the order of analysis which he pursued, the theories of management were set and the theological/Biblical material was "stretched" to fit the frame already in place. At a very fundamental level it appears to us that this ordering of the process raises serious question about the enterprise. The "master" being served appears to be the administrative theory to which Rudge is already committed. However, even given this major flaw, Rudge has performed a significant service in

revealing at a more than superficial level the serious work needed to find valid ways in which the secular insights from management thought and practice can be incorporated into our understanding and our functioning as faithful ministers. He has helped us to become more serious about our stewardship of knowledge, both theological and managerial.

34. For a discussion of the various management theories, see the following: Max Weber, *The Theory of Social and Economic Organization,* tr. by A. M. Henderson and Talcott Parsons (Free Press, 1947); Amitai Etzioni, *Modern Organizations* (Prentice-Hall, 1964); Dalton E. McFarland, *Management: Principles and Practices,* 4th ed. (Macmillan Publishing Co., 1974); William G. Scott, "Organization Theory," in Henry L. Tosi, *Theories of Organization* (St. Clair Press, 1975); Tom Burns and G. M. Stalker, *The Management of Innovation* (London: Tavistock Publications, 1961); Harold Koontz, "The Management Theory Jungle," *Journal of the Academy of Management,* Vol. 4, No. 3 (Dec. 1961), pp. 174–188; Harold Koontz, "Making Sense of Management Theory," *Harvard Business Review,* July-Aug. 1962, pp. 24–30; and Daniel A. Wren, *The Evolution of Management Thought* (Ronald Press Co., 1972).

35. Max Weber, *The Protestant Ethic and the Spirit of Capitalism,* tr. by Talcott Parsons (London: George Allen & Unwin, Ltd., 1930).

36. C. H. Dodd, *The Interpretation of the Fourth Gospel* (Cambridge University Press, 1968), p. 143.

37. Niebuhr, *Christ and Culture,* pp. 196–206.

38. Ibid., p. 192.

39. Ibid., p. 193.

40. Ibid., p. 195.

41. Ibid., p. 201.

42. Ibid., p. 205.

43. E. F. Scott, *The Fourth Gospel* (1908), p. 115; quoted in Niebuhr, *Christ and Culture,* p. 205.

44. An official statement from a World Council of Churches paper quoted in *Time,* Oct. 2, 1978, p. 46.

45. McNeill, *The History and Character of Calvinism,* pp. 184–185.

46. Thomas McCrie, *The Life of John Knox* (Glasgow: Free Presbyterian Publications, 1976), pp. 159–163.

47. Ibid., pp. 112–113.

48. Tillich, *Systematic Theology,* Vol. III, p. 14.
49. Ibid., p. 15.
50. Ibid., p. 30.
51. Ibid., pp. 196f.
52. Ibid., pp. 212f.
53. Ibid., p. 214.
54. Ibid., pp. 214–215.
55. Ibid., p. 216.
56. In 1937, Ludwig von Bertalanffy, the University of Chicago biologist, introduced into his seminars the notion of a "general systems theory." He utilized "models" which would describe interrelationships in the real world between the various organisms studied by a variety of sciences and disciplines. Norbert Weiner in 1948 coined the term "cybernetics" to describe ways in which information in "feedback loops" can be utilized to control various systems and mechanisms. Kenneth Boulding in 1956 sought to put the work of these two and others into a general theory with nine levels of systems for analysis listed in order of ever-increasing complexity from simple static frameworks, through more complex thermostatic cybernetic levels, up to the complexities of the human and social organizations, and finally labeled the ninth and most complex level as the "transcendental" level. The development of the computer in the last twenty years has given systems theorists a powerful tool in seeking to put into practice the theories that had been developing. It made possible very sophisticated development of information systems, mathematical models, simulation and game theory. "These specialized areas of study were evolving (in management thought) toward more and more of a 'systems approach' until 'systems' was to become *the* catch phrase of the modern era." (Wren, *The Evolution of Management Thought,* pp. 480–492.)
57. Ibid., p. 486.
58. *Interpreter's Dictionary of the Bible,* Vol. II, p. 73.
59. Hans von Campenhausen, *Ecclesiastical Authority and Spiritual Power in the Church of the First Three Centuries,* tr. by J. A. Baker (Stanford University Press, 1969), pp. 76–123.
60. Ibid., p. 293.
61. Ibid., p. 294.
62. Ibid., p. 296.
63. Ibid., p. 80.
64. Floyd V. Filson, *A Commentary on the Gospel According to*

St. Matthew, Harper's New Testament Commentaries (Harper & Row, 1961).

65. Ibid., p. 4.
66. Ibid., p. 20.
67. Ibid., p. 29.
68. Ibid.
69. Tillich, *Systematic Theology,* Vol. III, p. 80.
70. Ibid.
71. Wren, *The Evolution of Management Thought,* p. 415.
72. Harold Koontz and Cyril O'Donnell, *Essentials of Management,* 2d ed. (McGraw-Hill Book Co., 1978), pp. 59f.
73. Niebuhr, *The Purpose of the Church and Its Ministry,* p. 27.
74. For a more extended discussion of "premising," see Koontz and O'Donnell, *Essentials of Management,* pp. 71–73 and 149–150.
75. See the discussion of "centeredness" and the leader, under the heading "The Minister as Person," in Chapter I, above.
76. Early work on this book took place in England in 1978, during the period when the Roman Catholic Church was forced by events of human death to select two successive bishops of Rome within a two-month time span. Both of those elected emphasized simple personal acts that symbolized their personal unease with the traditional emphasis on the authority and grandeur of the office. Also, one has only to visit a few of the "Bishop's Palaces" that remain on the English landscape to sense in great detail what some periods of history have supported in terms of episcopal position. The builders and residents of those palaces were indeed "princes" in every sense of the term!
77. In this understanding of the Gospel of Mark we depend upon the analysis of Howard Clark Kee in his book *Community of the New Age* (Westminster Press, 1977). Kee has developed a method for studying Mark which incorporates an interrelation of social, literary, and conceptual modes of examination. The result of his work is the portrayal of Mark as a Gospel foundation for a sectarian community which believes that a new kingdom has been inaugurated, but which is also waiting for a promise that has yet to be fulfilled. The community saw itself in conflict with established secular and religious authority, and it saw its message as going forth only if it stood fast to its responsibilities in the face of the temptations of compromise. While these responsibilities do not mean withdrawal and exclusivism, they do mean a near-total lack of commu-

nity organization and a strong sense of standing over against the world. In this sense the Gospel of Mark can serve a paradoxical role in relation to a discussion of the office of bishop.

78. Tillich, *Systematic Theology,* Vol. III, p. 83.

79. We base this outline of the discussion on MBO primarily upon the work of Arthur X. Deegan II and Roger Fritz, *MBO Goes to College* (University of Colorado Press, 1975).

80. Arthur X. Deegan II, *Management by Objectives for Hospitals* (Germantown, Md.: Aspen Systems Corporation, 1977), p. 37.

81. Don Hellriegel and John W. Slocum, Jr., *Management: Contingency Approaches* (Addison-Wesley Publishing Co., 1974), p. 234.

82. Ibid.

83. Lindgren and Shawchuck, *Management for Your Church.*

84. A helpful presentation on charting which informs this discussion is found in John M. FitzGerald and Ardra F. FitzGerald, *Fundamentals of Systems Analysis* (John Wiley & Sons, 1973), pp. 227–263.

85. *Concise Oxford Dictionary of Current English* (Oxford: Clarendon Press, 1969).

86. Tillich, *Systematic Theology,* Vol. III, pp. 185–187, 193–196.

87. Ibid., p. 186.

88. Ibid., p. 187.

89. G. H. P. Thompson, *The Gospel According to Luke,* New Clarendon Bible Series (Oxford: Clarendon Press, 1972), p. 13.

90. G. B. Caird, *Saint Luke,* Westminster Pelican Commentaries (1963; Westminster Press, 1977), p. 14.

91. Niebuhr, *The Purpose of the Church and Its Ministry.*

92. Gerhard von Rad, *Old Testament Theology,* tr. by D. M. G. Stalker, Vol. II (Harper & Row, 1965), pp. 50–53.

93. See "Administration: The Centripetal/Centrifugal Gift," in Chapter I, above.

94. See the annual reports to the George D. Dayton Foundation for the years 1976, 1977, and 1978, and the "Final Evaluation Report for Viable Futures for Congregations Project," Dec. 3, 1976 (unpublished).

95. Wesley J. Visey, "A Curriculum for a Theological Seminary," *Christian Advocate,* Sept. 29, 1960, as reprinted in *Seminary Quarterly,* Winter 1961–62.

96. "Integrating Disciplines," in Chapter I, above.

97. "Biblical Insights on Bishops" and "Order and Anarchy" in Chapter IV, above.

98. Niebuhr, *Christ and Culture,* p. 227.